more...

a 40-day devotional journey
through depression and anxiety

Chris Beam

Contents

introduction
Day 1 – "No. And if you do…"
Day 2 – You Are with Me
Day 3 – 40 Days in the Desert
Day 4 – the Broken Hearted
Day 5 – Every Thought Captive
Day 6 – Abundance of the Heart
Day 7 – Enough of Its Own
Day 8 – Man of Sorrows
Day 9 – Consider It All Joy
Day 10 – Letting Go of Resentment
Day 11 – Rejoice
Day 12 – Comfort One Another
Day 13 – Comfort My People
Day 14 – In the Belly of a Great Fish
Day 15 – Grace after Grace
Day 16 – Demolishing Strongholds
Day 17 – Love One Another Deeply
Day 18 – I Shall Not Want
Day 19 – The God of Peace
Day 20 – Be Strong and Courageous
Day 21 – A New Heart
Day 22 – You Can Handle the Truth
Day 23 – A New Song
Day 24 – Under Pressure
Day 25 – a sad face
Day 26 – A Time for Laughter
Day 27 – O My Soul

Day 28 – It Is What It Is

Day 29 – Crossroads

Day 30 – Think on These Things

Day 31 – Hold the Line

Day 32 – The Power Within

Day 33 – ir·ri·ta·ble

Day 34 – Be

Day 35 – whatever

Day 36 – too much, too little, too late

Day 37 – Run the Race

Day 38 – First Things First

Day 39 – No Room for Grace

Day 40 – The Good Shepherd

introduction

We want more. If you're battling depression or anxiety, you want more than what you are now experiencing. You want more than just surviving. We were made for more. We were made to be in intimate relationship with the God of all the universe, the God who created everything. We were created to know Him in all of His vastness. And then we settle into our comfortable lives and focus on life. We shouldn't settle for less.

When Jesus was asked what the most important commandment was, He responded, *"'Hear, O Israel: The Lord our God, the Lord is one. Love the Lord your God with all your heart and with all your soul and with all your mind and with all your strength.' The second is this: 'Love your neighbor as yourself.' There is no commandment greater than these."* (Mark 12:29-31)

Jesus told us the most important thing that God, the Creator of everything, instructed us to do is to love Him with our whole hearts, with everything we are. And then He explained, we are to love our neighbor as we love ourselves. Love Him with everything we are. This was not a commandment just for those who were doing well or who had the time, it was a commandment to all of us regardless of what we are going through. Depression and anxiety have a way of affecting "everything we are"; they impact us on every level.

Depression and anxiety are more than just feeling sad or stressed. We almost do a disservice by naming clinical disorders after emotions. It sounds like we are only talking about how we feel. They affect us on every level: emotional, spiritual, cognitive, physical, and relational - with all our heart, soul, mind, strength, and our 'neighbor as ourselves'. To only address the emotional aspect would leave out so much of what depression and anxiety are. And because these levels are so integrated, we have to address each level.

For some, depression and anxiety hit for a season and then we move on, we move out of it. For others, depression and anxiety can settle in for years, drastically impacting our lives and the lives of those around us. We feel overwhelmed, exhausted, alone, defeated, discouraged, or in a fog. Even for believers, this can be discouraging. We know that God is there, that He cares, that He has a plan for our lives, and that He answers prayer and yet we may begin to wonder where is He in the midst of all that is going on. Whether it has been formally diagnosed or not, depression or anxiety can interrupt our lives daily but we also know that scripture promises *more* than what we are currently experiencing.

This 40-day devotion is not a quick-fix guide to magically erase the emotional struggles you may be going through but a way to find strength, encouragement, and hope through these difficult times. It is a daily walk through scripture to see how the God of peace can restore peace and hope.

Be willing to seek out a trained professional or a pastor if your thoughts are suicidal or you are thinking of causing harm to your self or someone else. There is no shame in seeking out the help you need.

The journey may turn around suddenly or it may press on beyond these forty days. My encouragement to you is to spend time daily in prayer and God's Word. Be intentional to examine how depression and anxiety are impacting you and your reaction to them. Allow Him to refresh and restore your anxious soul at a deep level. Ask Him to help you stand firm against these struggles that feel overwhelming. Let Him be your peace and joy. Listen and obey as He reveals His truth into areas of your life that need to change. Allow Him to lead you into *more*…

Day 1

This is the day which the LORD has made; Let us rejoice and be glad in it.

Psalm 118:24 (NASB)

Today, my focus is on You. Regardless of what is going on, I have to start somewhere. Let this be the starting point: to rejoice and be glad. When my eyes are on my circumstances this is hard to do but my hope is not on my ability to candy-coat everything and be fake. My hope is in You. This is the day that You have made.

The NIV translates this, "The Lord has done it this very day; let us rejoice today and be glad." He has done it. We can choose to focus on the pain of the past or the fears of the future or we can focus on Him today. He is our hope. When we struggle to believe this, His truth is still truth. David knew what it was like to experience fear and depression that appeared insurmountable. He knew those times when it seemed easier to fall over and not get back up. •

"When hard pressed, I cried to the Lord; he brought me into a spacious place. The Lord is with me; I will not be afraid. What can mere mortals do to me? The Lord is with me; he is my helper. I look in triumph on my enemies. It is better to take refuge in the Lord than to trust in humans. It is better to take refuge in the Lord than to trust in

princes.

All the nations surrounded me, but in the name of the Lord I cut them down. They surrounded me on every side, but in the name of the Lord I cut them down. They swarmed around me like bees, but they were consumed as quickly as burning thorns; in the name of the Lord I cut them down. I was pushed back and about to fall, but the Lord helped me. The Lord is my strength and my defense; he has become my salvation. Shouts of joy and victory resound in the tents of the righteous: 'The Lord's right hand has done mighty things! The Lord's right hand is lifted high; the Lord's right hand has done mighty things!' I will not die but live, and will proclaim what the Lord has done. The Lord has chastened me severely, but he has not given me over to death."

(Psalm 118:5-18)

"He has not given me over to death." It's hard to find hope when our minds seem to be working against us. Negative, self-defeating thoughts run out of control. Our emotions get stuck in second gear and won't shift. We lose trust and faith in those closest to us. The smallest task seems like climbing a mountain. And we wonder if we'll ever be ourselves again. Just like David, we can agree He has not given us over to death. Not yet. We still have today.

We have today and today is the day the Lord has made. What will we do with it? David felt the pressure but chose to move forward, "all the nations surrounded me… they surrounded me on every side, but in the name of the Lord I cut them down… I was pushed back and about to fall but the Lord helped me." He made a choice of what he would do. He chose to rejoice.

So Samuel took the horn of oil, anointed him in the presence of his brothers and the Spirit of the Lord took control of David from that day forward.

(1 Samuel 16:13 HCSB)

When we first hear of David in 1 Samuel 16, he is a young shepherd boy about to be anointed as king. That day changed the direction of his life. Verse 13 tells us, "and from that day on the Spirit of the Lord came powerfully upon David" (NIV). He was not the same from that day forward. He experienced life's whirlwinds: victories and tragedies, births and deaths, throne rooms and caves, leading armies and being chased by armies, elation and fear. We read of his emotional struggles through the Psalms but he knew where his hope and strength were found. From that day forward he was not the same; the Lord was with him.

There is a great scene in Peter Jackson's *The Hobbit: An Unexpected Journey* when Gandalf challenges Bilbo on why he is so resistant to the journey. Bilbo was content where he was and not looking for change. He was comfortable. Gandalf questioned, "When did doilies and your mother's dishes become so important to you?" Gandalf urged him on, "you'll have a tale or two of your own to tell when you come back." "...Can you promise that I will come back?" Bilbo wondered. "No. And if you do... you will not be the same," explained Gandalf. That is the challenge before us: will we stay the same or are we willing to be transformed by what He is doing in us? There is no promise we will come back. No promise that everything will be nice and easy and wonderful. That was never His promise to us.

We have a choice to find joy and a reason to rejoice in the middle of the depression and anxiety. Rejoicing is a different way of reacting to life's difficulties. It feels like too much work and we wonder if it is really worth it. If our goal is to stay the same then it is not worth it. We will keep doing and feeling the same things we have been doing and feeling. But, if we're willing to be transformed and we understand that He is using what we are currently going through, we will do something different. It may mean giving up some of what is comfortable and familiar and it will involve transformation. David declared the Lord has done it, "the Lord's right hand has done mighty things."

If nothing else, I choose to focus on You today. You are my hope. I lose nothing by believing You will help me, You are with me. I can choose to keep my eyes and my hope on You and what You have done. Each day, each journey begins with taking small steps. I'll keep moving forward, believing You are

1/31/17

able to handle what happens today. I'll rejoice in
Your great deeds.

"Therefore,
with minds that are alert
and fully sober,
set your hope on the grace
to be brought to you
when Jesus Christ
is revealed at his coming."
(1 Peter 1:13)

Lord, I lift up today to You and surrender the next
40 days. Open my eyes to Your truth and Your
reality. Transform my heart and mind to believe what
You say about me. As I face today, help my mind to
be fully alert and focused. Today, I choose to rejoice
and be glad that I have a today. My lips may not be
able to smile, my brain may not believe it, and my
body may not have the energy to move but I will
rejoice in You today. My goal is to not stay the same.

Day 2

Save me, O God, for the waters have come up to my neck. I sink in the miry depths, where there is no foothold. I have come into the deep waters; the floods engulf me. I am worn out calling for help; my throat is parched. My eyes fail, looking for my God... Answer me, Lord, out of the goodness of your love; in your great mercy turn to me.   Psalm 69:1-3,16

The Lord was with David. The Lord was with Joseph. The Lord was with Gideon. The Lord was with Joshua. God's promise to Moses was that He would be with him. It is what the angel spoke to Mary, "the Lord is with you." Jesus promised us, "Lo, I am with you always, even to the end of the age." (Mt. 28:20b NASB) He intended for us to go through life connected to Him. At very specific times, He spoke to individuals and to nations saying, "I am with You". We read consistently the Lord was with His people.

David's cry was for God to turn to him. God is with us. This is not based on feelings or something we tell ourselves just to feel better. It is His promise to us. It is a recurring theme throughout the Old and New Testament. From the very beginning, God reached out to His creation with this message, "I will be your God; you will be my people. I will be with you."

Even though I walk through
the valley of the shadow of death,
I fear no evil, for You are with me;
Your rod and Your staff,
they comfort me.
[(Psalm 23:4 NASB)]

Depression has a way of stealing our joy and leaving us feeling all alone. It's easy to think no one cares, no one is there, and no one understands. This is the time to challenge those self-defeating thoughts that tell you there is no hope. Believe He is with you. Believe that whatever you face today, God is with you. He has not abandoned you. Challenge that voice inside that says you are alone and that nothing will change.

We hear David's experience, as he felt defeated, overwhelmed, and outnumbered. *"Out of the depths I cry to you, Lord; Lord, hear my voice. Let your ears be attentive to my cry for mercy. If you, Lord, kept a record of sins, Lord, who could stand? But with you there is forgiveness, so that we can, with reverence, serve you. I wait for the Lord, my whole being waits, and in his word I put my hope."* (Psalm 130:1-5)

If we knew without a doubt God is with us then there is nothing we would not be able to face today. He is not calling us to anything more difficult than what He called Noah to, or Moses, or Abraham, or Joseph, or Mary, or Gideon. He was with each of them and He is with us. He has given you His Spirit to live in you, to empower you, and to equip you to face whatever it is you are going through. He may not chase the storm away but He will give you a way through it. And He will be with you through it. As dark and hopeless as it may feel, He is with you.

*Help, God — the bottom
has fallen out of my life!
Master, hear my cry for help!
Listen hard! Open your ears!
Listen to my cries for mercy.*
(Psalm 130:1,2 The Message)

One of the wonders of our faith is that God will be with us regardless of the struggle we face. He is more than able to handle whatever it is we are gong through. He has not left us or abandoned us. We shouldn't overlook or minimize God's presence with us. He doesn't overlook it. He promises to be with us, to live in us, to never forsake us. He is with us always. He is faithful to dwell in us and empower us to do what He is calling us to.

Is He is calling us to anything greater than what He called them to? They were called to free His people, to settle the Promised Land, to kill the giant, to defeat the enemies, to bring down the walls, to overcome that which stood against them.

We think it's a special occasion when we hear God was with David, with Gideon, or with Joshua but He promises to be with each of us. Immanuel, God with us, it's no coincidence. Jesus came to reconcile us to the Father. Be assured the Lord is with you.

1/6/17

[What are you facing today that you can't overcome with His presence?] What are you facing today that you won't be able to accomplish if the Lord is with you?

God, help me to find my strength in You. Let my strength be the strength of Your might. Help me to remember throughout the day that I am not alone, You are with me. Whatever I face today, I can endure and overcome with Your strength. Help me to learn what it really means to put my hope in You.

A Word of Hope for Today: the voice of depression and anxiety can be a message of fear and defeat and rejection. Challenge those thoughts and replace them with God's truth. His word says He is with you. That is the mission for today – let your response to every negative thought or emotion be "He is with me."

He is with me!

Adapted from 6:27, p. 247, *interference* by Chris Beam. (2014)

Day 3

Remember how the Lord your God led you all the way in the wilderness these forty years, to humble and test you in order to know what was in your heart, whether or not you would keep his commands. He humbled you, causing you to hunger and then feeding you with manna, which neither you nor your ancestors had known, to teach you that man does not live on bread alone but on every word that comes from the mouth of the Lord. Your clothes did not wear out and your feet did not swell during these forty years. Know then in your heart that as a man disciplines his son, so the Lord your God disciplines you.   Deuteronomy 8:2-5

There are those times when it seems like we get hit from every side, blow after blow. It makes us question our value, meaning, and purpose. There are a lot of unanswered questions. Why me? Why now? Why am I going through this? Why am I going through this again? Why doesn't He hear? Why doesn't He care? Why doesn't He answer? Why doesn't He stop this?

The Lord spoke to the Israelites as they wandered in the desert. They had those questions. He spoke to them as they were about to cross the Jordan into the Promised Land. He explained that their time in the desert was for discipline, for training. The Promised Land had struggles and temptations of its own and He was preparing them. *The grass seems greener on the other side.* The Promised Land was a land flowing with milk and honey but it also came with threats. There were battles to fight as they conquered other nations. There were temptations of compromise and complacency. The Israelites had to continue to trust in the Lord to remain a people set apart for Him. They were out of the frying pan and into the melting pot, surrounded by other cultures and gods that would lure them away and dilute their faith. Their time in the desert was the result of bad choices but God used it to prepare them for what came next. He did it to humble them, test them, and teach them.

It's easy to think, in the middle of the desert, that you can't take any more. Be encouraged. Know that God is using this time to train you and equip you. It may be hard to find joy, difficult to be hopeful, and your strength may be gone. God did not abandon His people in the desert. In spite of their sin, He did not forsake them. Through a cloud by day and a pillar of fire by night, He led them. Listen for Him to lead You - through His word, through quiet times of prayer and submission, through the encouragement of other believers, or through the gentle leading of His Spirit within you.

The Promised Land was not a vacation in paradise. It had it's own struggles. The Israelites had to fight battle after battle to defeat the inhabitants of the land they were taking. They had to be obedient as they continued to rely on the Lord. When they weren't in battle, they were enticed with the gods and strange ways of the people they lived among. They had to constantly be on their guard against compromise and convenience.

Humble yourselves, therefore,
under the mighty hand of God,
so that He may exalt you
at the proper time,
casting all your care on Him,
because He cares about you.
(1 peter 5:6,7 HCSB)

Be prepared to fight the battles to claim the land. His goal is not to make you comfortable but to make you holy. He is using this time now to shape your character to prepare you for what's coming next. Through it all He is with you. There is something coming after this or while you are still going through this. It will happen. And just as sure as you are that something else will happen, you can be confident that He will be with you through this but He is also using this to prepare you and equip you for that. The time in the desert has a purpose. His goal may not be to get you out of the desert but to be with you as you cross through it.

Be honest about the doubts and fears you have. Cast your cares on Him because He cares for you. If you're not sure you'll make it through or you're struggling to believe He is with you; confess that. It's a great place to start by recognizing the hurt and pain and fear that is there.

Lord God, You reign. Help me to surrender completely to Your will, to Your mercy and compassion. These dry times are chipping away at my joy, my hope, my life. I know that You desire more for me than to let depression or anxious thoughts steal my joy. I don't want to be defined by this desert. I want to be defined and encouraged in who You say I am and what You are doing in me.

A Word of Hope for Today: Challenge the distorted thoughts that tell you there is no hope, that you are not enough. Especially challenge those thoughts that repeatedly tell you it's supposed to be easy or fair, that your life is supposed to be happy all the time, that others have it better than you, that God must be punishing you, or that He is not there for you. Replace it with His truth.

Day 4

The Lord builds up Jerusalem; he gathers the exiles of Israel. He heals the brokenhearted and binds up their wounds. He determines the number of the stars and calls them each by name. Great is our Lord and mighty in power; his understanding has no limit. The Lord sustains the humble but casts the wicked to the ground.

Psalm 147:2-6

He knows we are but dust. We are dependent on His grace and mercy. Whether we believe it or accept it, it is true. He sustains us. He binds up our wounds and heals our broken hearts.

I don't know what your pain is but it's there. Depression and anxiety have a way of festering in those open wounds. If we allow it, depression, fear, worry, anger, and resentment grab a foothold in the pain we experience.

Sometimes it is the result of hurt and pain caused by others. Their unhealthy, inconsiderate choices wound us. Sometimes, it's our poor choices that bring the pain. Sin brings death, separation, and deep wounds. And sometimes it's no one's fault, life just happens, we live in a fallen world. The storms hit when we're not looking.

God puts the fallen on their feet again
(Ps. 147:6a The Message)

The Message interprets verse 6 as "God puts the fallen on their feet again" - He puts us upright, He heals our pain. He comes to our rescue. He is very aware of what we are going through. I like that verse 3 says, "He heals the brokenhearted and binds up their wounds." I know I need healing. God knows this too.

He does more than just make us feel good, He heals our wounds. He brings healing to deep sadness that covers our soul. Sometimes we just want to feel better, we want the pain to stop but He goes deeper than that, He heals us. This healing takes time because it has a greater purpose.

When we settle for just wanting to feel better, we miss out on how He shapes and molds our character through this suffering. We sidestep His holiness. Surgery hurts. It's different than just being cut, it has a purpose – to take out what is bad - but we have to be cut open during the process. We often want to skip the surgery because there is pain involved, it takes time to recover, it interrupts our lives, it costs money, it may not produce the results we're looking for, there are no guarantees, we can't control it. With surgery, we put our unconscious bodies into the hands of a (hopefully) capable and trustworthy surgeon. He will make decisions based on what is best for our well-being and we have to trust he knows what is best. His goal is not just to make us emotionally feel better but to make us healthier, whole, complete. The surgeon may just be in it for the money but I want to believe he cares that we get better.

He determines

the number of the stars

and calls them each by name.

(Psalms 147:4 HCSB)

How loved do you feel? In your heart of hearts, do you honestly believe He cares for you? Don't give the safe, Sunday-school answer, the answer that "good" Christians are supposed to respond with - do you feel loved? This is not a question of whether you know God loves everyone and you fall into that "everyone" category but have you experienced freedom, fullness, and joy in His presence? In spite of the hurt, have you experienced some of the healing? Is there something in your past that convinces you over and over again that it just isn't true, or at least, not for you? Are there circumstances that your mind keeps pointing to as proof that God is not real or doesn't care, at least not real or caring in your life? Can you dare to believe that He wants to heal you and He does care for you? Do you fit into that category of the "brokenhearted"?

He heals the brokenhearted

and binds up their wounds.

(Psalms 147:3 HCSB)

The psalmist was speaking of Israel in captivity as he wrote this passage. The generations before him had been in and out of captivity and bondage but God brought the exiles back. It happened repeatedly as Israel strayed from the Lord. He allowed them to make their choices but He also responded to their cries for help. The captivity lasted years, Jerusalem was attacked, the city walls were torn down, and the people were scattered. God didn't stop caring and He didn't give up but He did allow their choices.

Your days may be dark and friends may seem distant and uncaring. Your wounds may be deep and may not even be the result of your choices. Your hope may be gone and your strength dried up. Emotionally you may feel overwhelmed and defeated. His words to you are that He heals the brokenhearted and He binds up their wounds. Jesus suffered His own wounds and agony to bring us back to the Father. To bring us back from captivity. This may not be a question of whether you are a believer, are you saved, but a question of how you trust fully in His ability to redeem and restore you. Are you putting your life in His hands as He performs the surgery or do you keep snatching it back because you're not convinced He is the "good" shepherd?

Father, heal this broken heart, bind up these wounds that are emotional, relational, physical, spiritual, and mental. Bring wholeness and healing to this life. Help me to see You and hear You in new ways. Use this time of brokenness and healing to be a time of transformation. Rather than being a victim, help me to experience full meaningful life in You.

The Spirit of the Lord is on Me,
because He has anointed Me
to preach good news to the poor.
He has sent Me to proclaim
freedom to the captives
and recovery of sight to the blind,
to set free the oppressed,
to proclaim the year
of the Lord's favor.
(Luke 4:18,19 HCSB)

A Word of Hope for Today: It takes vulnerability and transparency to expose the wounds that are there. Name the hurt specifically. Admit that those wounds, those self-defeating thoughts, those intrusive fears and worries, or those pressing feelings of depression have impacted your life and in some ways controlled your life. Tell your Heavenly Father what the hurt is. Be obedient and courageous as He leads you to take steps of healing.

Are there times when you avoid the healing process, the surgery, because it is too uncomfortable, too painful, too risky, or too awkward? Are there times when you are more focused on feeling good rather than getting better?

Day 5

For though we walk in the flesh, we do not war according to the flesh, for the weapons of our warfare are not of the flesh, but divinely powerful for the destruction of fortresses. We are destroying speculations and every lofty thing raised up against the knowledge of God, and we are taking every thought captive to the obedience of Christ

2 Corinthians 10:3-5 (NASB)

Our minds are under attack. Verse 5 is rendered differently in different translations: speculations, every lofty thing raised up against the knowledge of God, pretensions, arguments, every high-minded thing, imaginations. These all allude to thoughts or patterns of thinking in opposition to what we know and understand about God. It is the battlefield of the mind.

Our fallen nature and our tendency towards sin leads to distortions in our perceptions. We tend to twist reality when we fill in the blanks with our assumptions. Even God's truth about Him and ourselves get reshaped by our experiences, our wounds, our resentment, our fears and anxiety, or dark depression.

The serpent said to the woman, "You surely will not die! For God knows that in the day you eat from it your eyes will be opened, and you will be like God, knowing good and evil." (Genesis 3:5,6 NASB)

But it's not just us. We have an adversary who twists the truth and accuses us. He accuses God. Satan is the father of lies. His goal is not for us to worship him, his goal is for us to not worship God. If he can distort our view of God, he is succeeding. We hear very clear in Genesis 3 how he re-interpreted God's instructions with Eve. He diluted God's truth with accusations to get Eve to believe God was holding back on what she was "entitled" to. We're under attack daily as we fall for the image that Satan paints of us. He would have us prideful and arrogant so we don't need God then guilt-ridden, defeated, and powerless when we are made new in Christ. He wants us to put our faith in ourselves not in Our Heavenly Father. He wants us to believe God isn't there, doesn't care, doesn't do anything, and is unaware. He wants us to be so distracted with petty problems, emotional wounds and scars, anger, resentment, and un-forgiveness that depression and anxiety seem natural. If he can get us focused on who has offended us and how they are the problem, we'll be consumed with that more than pursuing a holy God with all of our hearts. We fall for the lie that this depression will last forever, there's no point in trying, it will never get better, no one cares, and we would be better off dead. We give in to the fear of what could happen and listen to the voice that says we are not safe and everyone else's lives are a relaxing vacation in paradise.

These are the strongholds we allow to build up in our minds. They often start off as small footholds and turn into deeply entrenched vantage points. These are the strongholds we can tear down with God's power.

We are destroying speculations and every lofty thing raised up against the knowledge of God...
(2 Corinthians 10:5)

"For though we walk in the flesh, we do not war according to the flesh, for the weapons of our warfare are not of the flesh, but divinely powerful for the destruction of fortresses. We are destroying speculations and every lofty thing raised up against the knowledge of God, and we are taking every thought captive to the obedience of Christ." The Message says it this way, "fitting every loose thought and emotion and impulse into the structure of life shaped by Christ." We have to fight against the lie that depression and anxiety have to define us.

There is an unhealthy perpetuating cycle between those self-defeating thoughts, out of control emotions, and deflating behavioral patterns. Attack the strongholds. Believe you can change the patterns. Bring every thought captive in obedience to Christ. Who does He say you are? Not, who do you feel like you are or who have others verbalized you are or who have fear and insecurity turned you into. Who does God say you are?

Bring every thought captive in obedience to Christ. Start to catch and challenge those thoughts that say it will never change. Challenge those thoughts that assume you know what others are thinking or that you absolutely know their heart motives. Be honest with yourself that you can't read minds or see into the future or that you are always right and they are always wrong. Identify those thought patterns that play and replay over and over again.

And do not be conformed
to this world,
but be transformed
by the renewing of your mind, so
that you may prove
what the will of God is,
that which is
good and acceptable and perfect.
(Romans 12:2 NASB)

The good news is that He wants to transform you through the renewing of your mind. (Rom 12:2) He wants you to put your mind on things above, those things which are good, upright, and lovely. (Col 3, Phil 4) He knows you cannot do this on your own - He has given you His Spirit to live in you and to empower you. (Phil 2:13) *"You were taught, with regard to your former way of life, to put off your old self, which is being corrupted by its deceitful desires; to be made new in the attitude of your minds; and to put on the new self, created to be like God in true righteousness and holiness." (Ephesians 4:22-24 NASB)*

He made Him who knew no sin
to be sin on our behalf,
so that we might become
the righteousness of God in Him.
(2 Corinthians 5:21)

Satan twisted the truth with Eve. He told her God was holding back, that she wasn't like God and God didn't want her to be like Him. Before she and Adam fell for the lie, they were righteous; they were created in God's image. There was no sin separating them from God the Father. What we hear in scripture is that God wants us to know His good, acceptable, and perfect will. He wants us to be like Him in righteousness and holiness. He sent His Son to make us the righteousness of God. Sin brought with it separation and death, accusations and guilt, distance and fear. Fear and twisted thoughts turn us from Him rather than towards Him. *"So this I say, and affirm together with the Lord, that you walk no longer just as the Gentiles also walk, in the futility of their mind, being darkened in their understanding, excluded from the life of God because of the ignorance that is in them, because of the hardness of their heart." (Ephesians 4:17,18 NASB)*

Father, thank You for pursuing after me. Thank You that You value me and gave Your Son as a sacrifice for me. I am precious in Your sight. Help me to see that. Help me to challenge the thoughts that tell me I am worthless, You don't care, or my life is meaningless. Your Word says You have loved me with an everlasting love, You draw me with kindness, You call me Your own.

A Word of Hope for Today: Who does God say you are? What defines and identifies you? Find three scripture verses that tell you who you are in Christ. Write these out and put them on the bathroom mirror, on the fridge, by the front door, in the car. Keep your mind on these things. These are His truth about you.

Write out your thoughts after you have experienced extreme emotions of fear, anger, resentment, anxiety, stress, or depression. Don't write what you thought about, write what you actually said to yourself. Compare or contrast these thoughts with God's truth. Take the time to hear what you are saying to yourself and challenge those thoughts with God's truth.

Day 6

"No good tree bears bad fruit, nor does a bad tree bear good fruit. Each tree is recognized by its own fruit. People do not pick figs from thorn bushes, or grapes from briers. A good man brings good things out of the good stored up in his heart, and an evil man brings evil things out of the evil stored up in his heart. For the mouth speaks what the heart is full of."
Luke 6:43-45

"The mouth speaks what the heart is full of." Our words, our attitudes, our actions, and our thoughts reflect what is in our hearts. It's hard to think or speak positive when we're battling depression or overwhelmed with anxiety. Our thoughts can naturally gravitate towards the worst-case scenario – those negative, self-defeating beliefs that it will not get better.

For some people those beliefs go very deep, to the core. Life experiences and relationships shape, mold, and reinforce those beliefs or rules. These are not always bad or destructive. Sometimes these beliefs are positive messages, "I can be loved, I am valued, I can succeed, I am capable, people can love me, relationships are important, hard work = good things, God is good, etc..." Sometimes these core beliefs sound very different, "people will hurt you, I am not safe, I have to be perfect to be loved, I have to hurt you before you hurt me, trust no one, love =

pain." And because these life rules or beliefs are buried so deep we may be unaware how active they are in our lives. We don't see how they drive our choices or actions or self-talk. We want to be loved and accepted but that deep-seated message works against what we really want and need. We believe those messages, those core beliefs.

For the mouth speaks
what the heart is full of.
(Luke 6:45)

And then we speak: to others, about others, to ourselves, about ourselves, about God. We hear it and we believe it. We may know in our heads people care, we are loved, God is there and reaching out to us… but in our hearts it's a different story. We can know it but not believe it. After all, our failed relationships and our experiences of hurt and pain convince us of a different message. These beliefs become the filter through which we interpret and process the present circumstances, past experiences, and the future. We view others, ourselves, and God through this lens to tell us how it will affect us. And most of the time, that is our frame of reference – how it will affect me. God is good – *based on my experience of Him*. People can be trusted - *based on my experiences*.

God wants to transform us from the inside-out. He cares about the outside – our words, our behavior, how we treat others, and what we do. Many places in scripture directly tell us what behavior is acceptable, what we should or should not do. Our Heavenly Father also challenges us to be aware of our thoughts and how this affects us. We are instructed to keep our minds on things above, to bring every thought captive in obedience to Him, to think on those things which are good and upright, to be transformed by the renewing of our minds, and "with minds that are alert and fully sober, set your hope on the grace to be brought to you when Jesus Christ is revealed at his coming." (1 Peter 1:13) He wants to change not only our thoughts and actions but, more importantly, He wants to transform our hearts. Especially, our hearts.

" Moreover, I will give you

a new heart

and put a new spirit within you;

and I will remove

the heart of stone from your flesh

and give you a heart of flesh."

(Ezekiel 36:26 NASB)

He wants to transform our hearts with these beliefs that are grounded and shaped by pain, fear, anxiety, depression, selfishness, resentment, or sin. These core beliefs are formed through powerful experiences and meaningful relationships, good and bad. Some of us learned to trust others deeply because we were raised in safe, nurturing families. Some learned to open up and be vulnerable with others because there was a parent, a neighbor, a pastor, a coach, or a teacher who lived out what it means to really love and encourage. Some people develop that strong message of hope or faith not because of their circumstances but in spite of them. Others learned through unhealthy family environments to stay guarded and emotionally isolated. Some learned to be or appear "perfect" rather than resting in the sanctifying work of Christ. Some learned to work and push to achieve what they can never really achieve. Some heard the message, spoken and unspoken, over and over again, that they will never be good enough and this became their life motto. "The mouth speaks what the heart is full of."

> " The thief comes
> only to steal and kill and destroy;
> I came that they may have life,
> and have it abundantly."
> (John 10:10 NASB)

He wants to transform our hearts, to renew our minds, to restore our souls, to heal our wounds, to set us free from the bondage that says we have to do it all on our own. He wants to tweak those beliefs and set them inline with His truth.

Father, change my heart. Thank You for Jesus who died for me, who set me free, and gives me new life in You. Give me wisdom and discernment to see and hear those things which I cling to which are not of You. Help me to see what I really "believe" not just what I say I believe.

A Word of Hope for Today: There is hope. He has not forgotten you. He did not save you just to leave you the same – He wants to transform you.

Make a list of those things that you "believe". Be honest. When you hear yourself say things that you know are not in line with His word – write it down. Look for the patterns of how you perceive and interpret life, love, yourself, Him, or others. Scratch through the parts that are not truth and write in what is true.

Day 7

"For this reason I say to you, do not be worried about your life, as to what you will eat or what you will drink; nor for your body, as to what you will put on. Is not life more than food, and the body more than clothing? Look at the birds of the air, that they do not sow, nor reap nor gather into barns, and yet your heavenly Father feeds them. Are you not worth much more than they? And who of you by being worried can add a single hour to his life? And why are you worried about clothing? Observe how the lilies of the field grow; they do not toil nor do they spin, yet I say to you that not even Solomon in all his glory clothed himself like one of these. But if God so clothes the grass of the field, which is alive today and tomorrow is thrown into the furnace, will He not much more clothe you? You of little faith! Do not worry then, saying, 'What will we eat?' or 'What will we drink?' or 'What will we wear for clothing?' For the Gentiles eagerly seek all these things; for your heavenly Father knows that you need all these things. But seek first His kingdom and His righteousness, *and all these things will be added to you." So do not worry about tomorrow; for tomorrow will care for itself. Each day has enough trouble of its own."* Matthew 6:25-34

Jesus instructed us, "do not worry about your life." Easier said than done - but it is possible. We can do all things through Christ who strengthens us. Anxiety, doubt, and worry want us to focus on the problem not the solution. Anxiety rears its ugly head and tempts us to focus on the money and the bills and the hurt and the struggling relationship - it accuses us of not being enough, not having enough, not being good enough, and not able to make it through what we are facing. Why don't those nagging, reoccurring voices ever bring up the good things, the success stories?

Anxiety and worry are focused on tomorrow and next week and 10 years from now but God is focused on us right here, right now. He knows our needs. He knows our pain. He knows we are feeling the pressure and the pressure is very real. Jesus didn't say 'don't worry because there is nothing to worry about'. He said, "So do not worry about tomorrow; for tomorrow will care for itself. Each day has enough trouble of its own." He explained that our Heavenly Father knows what we need and He will supply what we need. He will supply what we need. He didn't tell us to paint over it or candy-coat everything because it doesn't matter – He actually acknowledged, "each day has enough trouble of its own."

> *" God will help you deal with whatever hard things come up when the time comes."*
>
> (Mt 6:34 The Message)

Jesus encouraged us to turn to Him, to seek the Father above everything else. Anxiety focuses on the problem. It tries to make us focus on our ability or inability to solve the problem so that our trust is more in us or our resources rather than in God. Eugene Peterson translates verse 34 this way, *"God will help you deal with whatever hard things come up when the time comes."* He wants to walk through this with us. Forty years in the desert for the Israelites was drudgery. It was the result of their choices but God used it to shape them and prepare them for the Promised Land, which had its own pressures and worries. He also used it as a time to walk with them, to lead them. Through the desert He was their God, they were His people, He was with them. There was a lot to worry about. They were not sure they would have enough to eat and they felt the fear and danger of impending attack. He supplied the bread. He protected them. He was their shield and their strength (Ps 7:10, Ps 28:7). He wants to walk with you through this.

You are probably tired of others telling you what to do to fix your problems or that your problems are not that bad or if you just have more faith it will all get better or go away. Sometimes, He takes it away. Sometimes, He chases away the storm. Sometimes He walks with us through it – to shape us and mold us but mostly for us to seek Him above everything. The storms can be very distracting. And the more distracting they are, the more we feel defeated and discouraged and hopeless.

" Are you not worth much more than they?"
(Mt. 6:26)

Jesus' answer for us is to trust God. Just because anxiety or depression make this hard to accept or believe, does not mean it is not the answer. He explained that God takes care of the birds in the air. He takes care of the lilies in the field. He tells us that our Heavenly Father will also take care of us. He tells us to have faith. Instead of seeking after all of the things we are anxious and worried about, we are to seek His kingdom, to seek after Him. This is not a magic combination to get God to move in our favor. This is not a secret password that unlocks the mysteries of the universe when we say it in just the right way at just the right time. It will not miraculously make all of our problems disappear. It is the way to work through whatever it is we are going through. We are to press on with Him rather than trying to creatively get Him to do it for us. We are to seek Him and His kingdom. Instead of what we can get from Him, we get Him. And, He is seeking after us. He pursues us and wants passionately to be with us. *"Are you not worth much more than they?"* He values us.

> *" For the pagans run after*
> *all these things,*
> *and your heavenly Father knows*
> *that you need them. "*
> (Mt. 6:32)

Worry indicates that our focus is on the object rather than Him. This does not mean that there aren't huge fears, worries, and stressors that need to be tackled. Real life is full of them. It does not mean that we don't have concerns. He tells us how to deal with these concerns. He knows that they are important to us and to Him. You may be working through a difficult relationship. You may be feeling abandoned, rejected, attacked, or wronged. You might be facing the darkest time of your life and you're not sure you will recover. Your Heavenly Father knows. Your Heavenly Father treasures you. Your Heavenly Father is asking you to trust Him to walk with you through this. He also knows that worrying will not change the conditions; it will only pile up more guilt, fear, or anxiety on you without solving anything. Worry will keep your eyes on you and what you are looking for rather than on Him.

> *" Can any one of you by worrying*
> *add a single hour to your life? "*
> (Mt. 6:27)

In the verses just before this, Jesus explained that we cannot serve two masters, *"either you will hate the one and love the other, or you will be devoted to the one and despise the other."* (v. 24) Our hearts were made to seek after one kingdom, one master. When we focus so much on our worries that it consumes us, we have taken our eyes off of Him. In verse 21, He pointed out that where our treasure is, our heart will be. When our hearts are divided, we are not seeking after His kingdom *first.*

" But seek first His kingdom
and His righteousness,
and all these things
will be added to you. "
(Mt. 6:33)

Father, show me where my heart is divided. Show me where I am consumed with building up my kingdom rather than seeking after Yours. Take this worry from me. I give it all to You. I trust You. I put my faith in You. With all that I am carrying, I trust You. I know You are faithful. You are good. You know what I need emotionally, financially, relationally, spiritually, physically, and mentally. I will trust in Your goodness and will seek Your kingdom first.

A Word of Hope for Today: Your Heavenly Father cares for you. He wants to provide for you. Identify the behavior that you do when anxiety starts to escalate. What do you do to feel better or fell less stressed? Do you avoid others, get defensive, go on the offensive, get angry, emotionally shut down, or stuff it all inside? Do you control others so you'll feel better?

Day 8

Isaiah 53:3-11 NASB

He was despised and forsaken of men, A man of sorrows and acquainted with grief; And like one from whom men hide their face He was despised, and we did not esteem Him. (v. 3)

Jesus knows our sorrow. He knows our struggle. He knows what it's like to be in a deep black hole and to feel like you'll never get out. Isaiah painted a picture of a hero who looked like *He* needed to be rescued. This isn't a picture of a dainty little Jesus with no dirt under his fingernails. Written about 700 years before Jesus was born, Isaiah accurately described the emotional, physical, mental, relational, and spiritual pain He suffered.

Though He was loved and followed by many who were close to Him, He experienced hurt, betrayal, rejection, ridicule, and personal attacks. The religious leaders attacked His character, beat His body, mocked His words, and humiliated Him in front of family and friends. He was found despicable and shameful. There was nothing of value to see in Him and they turned their faces from Him.

Surely our griefs He Himself bore, And our sorrows He carried; Yet we ourselves esteemed Him stricken, Smitten of God, and afflicted. (v. 4)

He was viewed as cursed and even rejected by

God. As He was beaten and crucified, He must have appeared foolish to have once proclaimed to be the Son of God. Where were the miracles now? Where was the power? The soldiers and the priests ridiculed Him, "He saved others, why can't He save Himself?" They wanted nothing to do with Him and saw no value in Him. You've had moments when you felt rejection and ridicule like that. Mistreated and misunderstood. The religious leaders didn't even believe God could love Jesus in that moment, "He trusts in God; let God rescue him if He delights in him." (Mt 27:43 NASB) Even the thieves hanging on crosses next to Him looked down on Him and hurled insults.

But He was pierced through for our transgressions, He was crushed for our iniquities; the chastening for our well-being fell upon Him, And by His scourging we are healed. (v. 5)

Pierced, crushed, chastened, and scourged. Other versions say wounded, ripped, disfigured, defiled. The Message says "there was nothing attractive about Him... He was looked down on and passed over... (He was thought of) as scum." Physically He was not much to look at. Others despised Him. You may be struggling with worth and meaning. Longing for others to see something of value in you. Or, you may have given up on that long ago - succumbed to that battle within, those voices that tell you to just give up, it will never change, there is no hope, you are nobody. You may be overwhelmed, feeling abused, defiled, disrespected, disfigured, abandoned, and lost. Your hurt goes deep and is a constant reminder that everything is not ok.

All of us like sheep have gone astray, Each of us has turned to his own way; But the LORD has caused the iniquity of us all to fall on Him. (v. 6)

He was innocent. Deserved none of what He experienced. Through an incredible act of mercy, He chose it. The Father poured on Him all that we deserve. We sin, we went astray, and He paid for it. Sometimes we experience pain, consequences, or deep wounds (physically, emotionally, relationally) because we make bad choices. Sin choices. The result of sin is death and brokenness. We hurt others: intentionally, unintentionally, directly, or indirectly. Even as believers, we are not immune to the results of our choices. We don't always see or care how our actions hurt others. Sometimes we are wounded and it had nothing to do with us. It was someone else's hurtful choices that wound us deeply and we carry that pain. Sometimes we let it define who we are. We may have been doing everything "right" - living responsible lives - and the choices of others drastically change the direction of our lives. We end up the one carrying the burden. Abuse, shame, guilt, and fear can be heavy loads to carry - especially when it was not the result of our choices. Sometimes it is the result of no one's choice. We live in a fallen world. Death, destruction, and decay happen. Even when we don't want it to. Illness and loss seem to rob us and we feel helpless at times.

He was oppressed and He was afflicted, Yet He did not open His mouth; Like a lamb that is led to slaughter, And like a sheep that is silent before its shearers, So He did not open His mouth. (v. 7)

He was afflicted with our pain, our sin, our choices, and our selfishness: the results of our "freedom". And He took it. He didn't object or back out. He took the full blow. "He did not open His mouth." He could have called legions of angels to stomp out the humans inflicting the pain but He remained silent. He could have stopped it before it ever began. He humbled Himself and became like us. Philippians chapter 2 says it this way, "Who, being in very nature God, did not consider equality with God something to be used to his own advantage; rather, he *made himself nothing* by taking the very nature of a servant, being made in human likeness. And being found in appearance as a man, he humbled himself by becoming obedient to death - even death on a cross!" (Phil 2:6-8 NIV)

By oppression and judgment He was taken away; And as for His generation, who considered that He was cut off out of the land of the living for the transgression of my people, to whom the stroke was due? (v. 8)

"He was cut off from the land of the living" because of our sin, our wrong-doing. He experienced death, painful death, but more than that, He experienced separation from God the Father. Separation from love and life and hope. We know what it feels like to be abandoned, neglected, hurt, rejected. To be with out hope. We have experienced the betrayal of others who were close to us. Jesus was attacked and accused and made to suffer for us and because of us. "By oppression and judgment, He was taken away." In that moment, they held power over Him, and they used it.

His grave was assigned with wicked men, Yet He was with a rich man in His death, Because He had done no violence, Nor was there any deceit in His mouth. (v. 9)

He was labeled as wicked. He knew what it meant to be judged by His outward appearance but also to be judged because of the hatred and biases of others that had nothing to do with him. He did not fit into their agendas. He was labeled and treated as the one who was wrong. We can recount those hurtful experiences when those closest to us found fault or ugliness in us because we don't fit into their picture of perfection, we make them uncomfortable and seem to "interfere" in their happy lives. They seem to hate who we are.

But the LORD was pleased To crush Him, putting Him to grief; If He would render Himself as a guilt offering, He will see His offspring, He will prolong His days, And the good pleasure of the LORD will prosper in His hand. (v. 10)

Crushed is not a good feeling. He felt the sense of loss, attack, and destruction of Himself as a person.

We have those moments of being crushed – emotionally, physically, mentally, relationally, or spiritually collapsed. We know those times when all of our hope has been snatched from us and it does not matter if it was because of our unhealthy patterns and distorted, self-defeating thoughts, because of insurmountable conditions, or because of the selfish attacks of others – the pain is still real, the wounds are still there, and the belief that it will get better has been ripped from our hearts.

As a result of the anguish of His soul, He will see it and be satisfied; By His knowledge the Righteous One, My Servant, will justify the many, As He will bear their iniquities. (v. 11) NASB

"He will see it and be satisfied..." We are made whole in Him. We are reconciled to the Father. We are justified and made right with God. All because of the anguish of His soul.

A Word of Hope for Today: He knows what it is like to feel crushed and defeated. He knows what it is like to face something you fear and dread with all your heart. He knows what it is like to feel you cannot go on. He knows what you are going through and He willingly endured His pain to set you free, to equip you and empower you, and to be able to walk with you through whatever it is you are facing.

Set three goals for today and accomplish them: go to the store, call the person you've been avoiding, go for a walk, read a chapter, etc... It may feel impossible, the anxiety may increase, but face the fear, be comfortable with being uncomfortable, take that step that you have been putting off. The medicine may not taste good but be willing to endure it.

Step outside the hurt or fear and ask yourself if there is something you are doing that hinders the work of God in you. Ask the Lord to search your heart. Make sure you are seeking Him and His kingdom rather than just what He can do for you.

> " looking unto Jesus, the author
> and finisher of our faith,
> who for the joy that was set before Him
> endured the cross, despising the shame,
> and has sat down at the right hand
> of the throne of God.
> For consider Him who endured such
> hostility from sinners against Himself,
> lest you become
> weary and discouraged in your souls."

(Hebrews 12:2,3 NKJV)

Father, I lift up today to You. You know the anguish of my soul. Give me the strength to do all You are calling me to do. Give me the strength and the courage to step out in faith and live boldly. Give me the strength to see what needs to change and to make those changes in me, in my relationships, in my behavior, in my innermost spirit. I cannot do this on my own – I cry out to You.

Day 9

But if any of you lacks wisdom, let him ask of God, who gives to all generously and without reproach, and it will be given to him. But he must ask in faith without any doubting, for the one who doubts is like the surf of the sea, driven and tossed by the wind. For that man ought not to expect that he will receive anything from the Lord, being a double-minded man, unstable in all his ways.

James 1:5-8

"Driven and tossed by the wind." This is not a good place to be. It's that place where it feels like nothing is easing up: bills to pay, aches and pains in your body, rejected and misunderstood by those who should be supportive, agonizing thoughts that won't let up, disappointment after disappointment, emotions that feel like their being whipped around in a hurricane, pressure to be or do something, and no energy or motivation to change any of it. Even if you knew what direction to go, you're not sure you could.

You may not even be sure where God is in the midst of this. Where is He today? Where is He right here, right now, in this moment? Does He care? This passage may feel more like condemnation being thrown at you – "for the one who doubts is like the surf of the seas, driven and tossed by the wind. For that man ought not to expect that he will receive anything from the Lord, being a double minded man, unstable in all his ways." But, this is God's truth about the state we are in when we don't believe He is the answer.

We hear His true heart in the previous verse, "…Let him ask of God who gives to all generously and without reproach, and it will be given to him." Generously and without reproach. He is not looking to trap us in our guilt and shame and hold it over us. He longs for us to call on Him. Even in the middle of the storm when we're feeling tossed back and forth, He wants us to turn to Him. Generously and without reproach. "Without reproach" – it's not a phrase we use a lot in English. It means it is done without the purpose of imposing shame, criticism, blame, or disgrace. He wants to respond to us in a way that is safe.

The answer to what we are going through may not come in the form or timing that we are looking for but He will come through. These verses are also building on the previous verses:

" Consider it all joy, my brethren, when you encounter various trials, knowing that the testing of your faith produces endurance. And let endurance have its perfect result, so that you may be perfect and complete, lacking in nothing."
(James 1: 2-4)

We will go through trials, struggles, temptations,

difficulties, and suffering. His encouragement to us is to consider all these struggles joyful. The NIV says to consider it "pure joy". The Message calls it "a gift" that we go through these difficult times because they are used to grow us. He may not take it all away but He will get us through it.

Perseverance and endurance are developed as we stand strong through these trials or storms. It almost seems backwards – don't we need perseverance or endurance to stand strong? Yes, but as we develop more fortitude through these struggles we also stand stronger in our faith, unwavering.

Ask boldly, believingly,
without a second thought.
People who " worry their prayers "
are like wind-whipped waves.
(James 1:6 The Message)

It may be hard to see or believe at this point but it is where our faith needs to be. We are to seek God for what we are to do through these circumstances and to ask in faith without doubting, without wavering. James' point is that doubting indicates that our faith is in more than one source. This is why we are tossed back and forth. Double-minded means we may believe God can do something but we are not convinced He will. Our minds are set on two (or more) "truths"; our faith is in God and… family, friends, money, our ability, ourselves, power, luck, etc… Double-minded is a mind set on two things not one; our hope sways back and forth and our lives reflect that double-mindedness. Our choices and lifestyles indicate where our hope really lies. Faith does not mean we will not experience depression, grief, or anxiety but it does determine how we will react to these. Endurance is not built by side-stepping the difficulties. We are made strong, whole, complete by pressing on through them. How will we react to the storms, the trials, the suffering?

Is your mind stayed on one course? Are there divided loyalties? Thoughts grounded in depression and anxiety tend to give us a distorted picture. Our ability to think clear decreases as our emotional intensity increases. The more stressed or depressed we are, the more our thoughts can be affected.

For as he thinks within himself,

so he is.

(Proverbs 23:7a NASB)

Not only do intense emotions affect what we think but they also affect how we think. It becomes more difficult to stay on task or to make simple decisions. We become easily distracted. We become more forgetful, more impulsive, more negative. We think more emotionally than rationally. And it becomes more difficult to stay single-minded as our thoughts become more scattered and more emotion driven. Two minds - rational and emotional, faith-based and fear-based, God-centered or me-centered.

Emotional reasoning is feeling based – what feels good. Impulsivity. Right and wrong become a matter of how we feel. Following God and His ways can become a question of how satisfying it feels. It's a really poor decision-making process. And, it's too erratic; our decisions change as our emotions change. *We may make a rash decision because we don't like how we feel, then we back step because we feel guilty and know that we're straying from God, but then that gets frustrating when we don't see results fast enough so we go in a different direction but then we wonder if God is there, does He really care, so we flip-flop and then we question why He would allow us to be jerked back and forth like this.* It tends to wear us out, leaving us more depressed or anxious.

Emotional reasoning can be much stronger than rational intellection. We can have all of the facts in front of us and know what the next right thing is but our hearts often trump our minds. Especially when it comes to love and relationships. Especially for the romantics among us who may have 38 solid reasons not to pursue the relationship and only one sliver of feeling to keep going but we'll follow our hearts every time. *We don't want to miss out on what God might be doing.* If you're not a romantic, this makes absolutely no sense at all. But that's part of the definition of romantic – it's not practical, not rational, not realistic. But, it's exciting (a feeling)… until it crashes.

Faith requires that we're romantics at times. Believing in something we cannot see is not practical or rational. Walking by faith is not realistic (according to the world's perception). But, there is a difference between putting our faith completely in God and being driven back and forth by unstable emotions.

If you don't know what you're doing,
pray to the Father.
He loves to help.
(James 1:5a The Message)

Father, help me to see You in the midst of the storm. Help me to be single-minded in how I react. Give me wisdom in the steps I take: how to react to others, how to be intentional to keep moving forward, how I spend my time, what I set my mind on, and how I perceive these struggles. You are my center. You are my strength.

A Word of Hope for Today: Your Heavenly Father longs to help you with what you are going through. He encourages you to bring your concerns to Him. Ask for His help; ask for wisdom and discernment to know what to do or how to do it. He won't shame you or mock you and He promises to respond.

What keeps you like "the surf of the sea, driven and tossed by the wind"? Name those things. Write out a list. Is it a person, a relationship, a fear, or insecurity? Do you have co-dependent relationships that you keep going and keep you going? Is there something or someone you treasure more than God?

Day 10

Be angry, and yet do not sin; do not let the sun go down on your anger, and do not give the devil an opportunity. He who steals must steal no longer; but rather he must labor, performing with his own hands what is good, so that he will have something to share with one who has need. Let no unwholesome word proceed from your mouth, but only such a word as is good for edification according to the need of the moment, so that it will give grace to those who hear. Do not grieve the Holy Spirit of God, by whom you were sealed for the day of redemption. Let all bitterness and wrath and anger and clamor and slander be put away from you, along with all malice. Be kind to one another, tender-hearted, forgiving each other, just as God in Christ also has forgiven you.

Ephesians 4:26 - 32 (NASB)

She said he didn't do what he should have done. She was talking about something that "didn't happen" 15 years ago. The tone of her voice made it clear there was resentment there. She wanted him to know… again, he was wrong. And wanted him to know God thought it was wrong.

As I listened to her recount the events, it seemed that this was not a matter of sin but a difference in perspectives. As we talked, I asked her if she thought it helped to hold on to this resentment - if this was what God wanted for her. This wasn't an issue of sin that needed to be dealt with but for her it was about hurt and pain that was buried deep. It was not a constant hindrance in their relationship but it was obviously still very real for her.

> " If a fellow believer hurts you,
> go and tell him — work it out
> between the two of you.
> If he listens, you've made a friend."
> (Mt 18:15 The Message)

I have a hard time believing that God wanted her to carry this burden of anger and bitterness for all these years. God didn't set her up to be the avenger of all wrongs. The guy may have been absolutely wrong for not coming through with what she thought he should have done – I wasn't there, I don't know. I do know her focus was on her expectations of what was 'supposed to be' rather than focusing on God working in her life through all of this.

A strong sense of truth and justice is difficult to battle. We don't want to let go of those wrongs, real or perceived. We like to think if we can show how wrong the other person is they will repent, apologize, change, love us more, value us more, or treat us better. It rarely happens that way. Especially when we hold on to that anger and bitterness for so long and (passive-aggressively) try to make them pay. We set them up to keep retaliating against us for what they perceive to be wrong on our part. It works better when we keep "short accounts" and go to the person humbly to talk about the conflict that comes between us.

This is hard to do. Especially when we are intent on maintaining our own kingdom and building it up so no one will ever hurt us again. Unresolved bitterness, anger, and resentment stuffed inside and turned inward often lead to disillusionment and depression. It's difficult to carry these things around knowing these wrongs have not been answered for. We try to work through it in our own strength, with our methods, but it doesn't work. This is why Paul wrote earlier in Ephesians 4: *"But you did not learn Christ in this way, if indeed you have heard Him and have been taught in Him, just as truth is in Jesus, that, in reference to your former manner of life, you lay aside the old self, which is being corrupted in accordance with the lusts of deceit, and that you be renewed in the spirit of your mind, and put on the new self, which in the likeness of God has been created in righteousness and holiness of the truth."* (v.20 – 24 NASB)

We are to "put on the new self, which in the likeness of God has been created in righteousness and holiness of the truth." Our old self relies on making others pay, proving them wrong, or believing we're not that bad (compared to others). God's reality is that we are made righteous and holy in Him. He saved us to transform us and part of that transformation is letting go of the wrongs done to us. Can I trust that God has a greater plan for me? Greater than any of those "plans" devised by hurtful people. In Genesis, Joseph learned this the hard way but realized what his brothers did to hurt him, God used for good (Gen 50:20). Our "truth and justice" is based on our ideas of right and wrong but God is transforming those into something new through grace and mercy.

Can we lay aside our resentment? It won't feel fair or right. Can we be angry and not sin? The anger and hurt are very real but hurting the other person or making them pay will not heal us. And it will not change them. In his letter to the Ephesians, Paul encouraged us to be angry but do not sin, to let our words build others up rather than tear them down, to show kindness to those who have hurt us, and to forgive them. This is asking a lot but it is steps towards healing. And we can't do this in our own strength.

He heals the brokenhearted and binds up their wounds.
(Psalm 147:3 NASB)

Father, You know the resentment and anger that I hide in my heart. You are not fooled by the smile on my face. Help me to walk in freedom. Help me to put on the new self - to see me as You see me. I can never be good enough to change this heart but through Your grace and mercy I am made new. I am made righteous and holy. Help me to respond to others in a holy way – with mercy and grace. I want to forgive others as You have forgiven me. In those moments when I want to lash out, help me to speak the truth in love, help me to go to others and work through the conflict. Father, You know the hurt that is buried there. You see how I hurt others so they wont hurt me. But it doesn't work. Heal these wounds. Bring peace and comfort and security which can only be found in You. Help me to see how I have hurt others. Show me who I need to go to and make things right.

A Word Of Hope for Today: Your Heavenly Father can restore what has been torn down. He can make it new again. He has already paid the price for the things you have done and the things done to you. Rather than keeping the wounds open and causing more pain, He wants to bring healing and freedom. Their past actions don't have to continue hurting you.

Name those you need to forgive. Write their names on a list and continue to pray daily for them. This may not seem right or fair but this is about your freedom and your healing not making them pay. Your anger is not an effective punishment on them, it's more of a punishment on you than on them. If you're holding on to resentment, believe He has already paid the price for their actions.

If there is someone you have hurt – go to them and make it right.

Day 11

Rejoice in the Lord always. I will say it again: Rejoice! Let your graciousness be known to everyone. The Lord is near. Don't worry about anything, but in everything, through prayer and petition with thanksgiving, let your requests be made known to God. And the peace of God, which surpasses every thought, will guard your hearts and minds in Christ Jesus. Philippians 4:4-7 (HCSB)

Rejoice. It's a verb, something we do or choose to do. Paul instructs us to rejoice and then he says it again. "Let your graciousness be known to everyone." This is actually the third time he repeats the instruction. According to Strong's Concordance, in the Greek, rejoice (xairo) means to be "favorably disposed" or "to find favor in". It comes from the same root word as grace (xairis). So when Paul encourages us to let our graciousness be seen by others, He is telling us to let others see that we are excited that we have experienced God's grace, His favor. Paul used the word 10 times the book of Philippians. The word is used 54 times in Psalms.

Be glad in the Lord and rejoice, you righteous ones; shout for joy, all you upright in heart.
(Psalms 32:11 HCSB)

Rejoice. It sounds like a religious word, a church word, formal, something that should be sung in 7-part harmony by a church choir. Paul called for believers to find joy in their circumstance. Not because of their circumstances but in spite of their circumstances. He told the believers to rejoice, to not worry about anything, to pray about everything, and to be thankful as they bring their requests or concerns to God. And then he explained, *"the peace of God, which surpasses every thought, will guard your hearts and minds in Christ Jesus."* (v.7) The peace is not there because we can solve every problem but because we can't. Our Heavenly Father is here with us, through it all, He shows us His favor: His peace will guard our hearts and minds. When our emotions are up and down and our thoughts are tossed back and forth, His peace, the peace that calms the storm inside of us, the peace that we cannot truly understand, the peace which is there when it should not be there, will be our calm assurance. His peace will calm that anxiety and fear that tell you it will not be ok. His peace can calm those voices inside that tell you you're not enough, you're not loveable, that no one values you. His peace will calm those depressing feelings and thoughts of dread and loneliness and defeat. His peace will guard your heart and your mind, if you choose it. It's not a magic blue pill that makes it all go away. It is peace and hope and faith, the assurance that as bad as the storm gets, your boat will not sink. And if it does sink, He will get you through it.

We wait for Yahweh;
He is our help and shield.
For our hearts rejoice in Him
because we trust in His holy Name.
(Psalm 33:20,21 HCSB)

To rejoice is the choice we make because we believe He is more than able to handle everything we are going through. It's what we choose on those days when we don't want to get out of bed. The days when we feel unlovable or unloved, mistreated, misunderstood, misled, and misguided. The days when our deepest fears keep us trapped in a cage of tears, or an apartment, or away from those who really do love us. He is our help and our shield, a strong tower to run to. More than just flowery religious words, Paul encouraged believers to take active steps of faith in troublesome circumstances. He was writing this letter from jail as he waited to hear if he would be put to death by soldiers. This was not a letter of defeat and surrender but an affirmation of his choice to rejoice in every circumstance.

Paul started off his letter to the Philippians with confidence and affirmation, *"In all my prayers for all of you, I always pray with joy because of your partnership in the gospel from the first day until now, being confident of this, that he who began a good work in you will carry it on to completion until the day of Christ Jesus."* (Philippians 1:4-6) Regardless of what happens or has happened, he knew that God would complete the work He was doing in other believers and in himself. Prison was not a detour from the process. And it should not be a distraction. Whatever the Philippian believers were experiencing was not a detour from the process. God was using it to complete the transformational work He was doing in them.

Paul continued the thought, *"And this is my prayer: that your love may abound more and more in knowledge and depth of insight, so that you may be able to discern what is best and may be pure and blameless for the day of Christ, filled with the fruit of righteousness that comes through Jesus Christ—to the glory and praise of God."* (Philippians 1:9-11) The work that God is doing in each of us will be completed and Paul prayed that the Philippian believers would know with a clear and insightful understanding "what is best". That they would not be blindsided or distracted by other things going on but would be able to discern what God was doing. And the result of this knowledge and discernment would be glory and praise to God. Rejoicing.

But what does it matter?

The important thing is that in every

way, whether from false motives or

true, Christ is preached.

And because of this I rejoice.

Yes, and I will continue to rejoice.

(Philippians 1:19)

In verse 12 Paul explained, *"Now I want you to know, brothers and sisters, that what has happened to me has actually served to advance the gospel."* It's probably not what he wanted or had planned, but being in prison became an opportunity. God was using this to complete the work in Paul but He was also using it to impact those around Paul.

Our reaction to hardship is often to look for the quickest route out. We should believe and bring all of these things to God in prayer. But, we can also pray for knowledge and discernment when God chooses to go in a different direction. Worship. Grow. Impact. As pastor Dean Inserra explains, God interferes in our lives for His glory, for our good, and for our neighbor. What we see as an interruption of our lives, He is using for our good. If He's using this, why would I go against this? Me struggling to get out of it will not work any way. My plans and schemes only mess it up worse.

"Rejoice in the Lord always. I will say it again: Rejoice! Let your gentleness be evident to all. The Lord is near. Do not be anxious about anything, but in every situation, by prayer and petition, with thanksgiving, present your requests to God. And the peace of God, which transcends all understanding, will guard your hearts and your minds in Christ Jesus." (Philippians 4:4-7 NIV)

You are the God of peace. You calm my anxious soul. I lift everything up to You, knowing You are more than able and so very willing to handle it all. I can trust You with everything. I choose to rejoice and praise and worship. Your glory is not diminished by my problems or attitude. I can rejoice in You.

A Word of Hope for Today: You have a choice: rejoice. Find the joy in every situation even when it does not seem to be there. Cover it with prayer. Believe, without doubting that God is able to overcome what you are going through. Ask for wisdom and discernment. Ask for strength and guidance. Be responsible. Take the steps He is leading you to take. If the circumstances continue, repeat.

Day 12

For when we came into Macedonia, we had no rest, but we were harassed at every turn — conflicts on the outside, fears within. But God, who comforts the downcast, comforted us by the coming of Titus, and not only by his coming but also by the comfort you had given him. He told us about your longing for me, your deep sorrow, your ardent concern for me, so that my joy was greater than ever.   2 Corinthians 7:5-7

Recently I was at a conference where the facilitator asked us to share examples of times when someone played the role of Titus in our lives. Everyone in the room had a story to share.

Hopefully, we've all had those experiences when someone came and shared just the right thing at just the right time. For the apostle Paul, it was Titus who brought words of encouragement and comfort. Paul was a missionary sharing the good news but was not always received with a warm welcome. He said he felt attacked from every side - "conflicts on the outside, fears within." He had been the target of believers and unbelievers. He pressed on through imprisonment, shipwrecks, beatings, and harassment. Now his young associate, whom he had ministered to, was ministering to him.

Blessed are those who mourn,
for they shall be comforted.
(Matthew 5:4 NASB)

Titus had traveled with Paul, had been impacted by his ministry, and had seen the difficulties of living out their faith in a radical way. He brought words of encouragement and hope. Even though our faith is in God, we can still be comforted by those around us. Paul recognized that "God, who comforts the downcast, comforted us by the coming of Titus". God used Titus in that opportunity to encourage Paul. God strengthened Paul through this encouragement at just the right time.

Sometimes we choose not to be comforted. We like playing the victim or the martyr; it keeps the focus on us and empowers us with emotional leverage. Sometimes, it's just more comfortable and familiar to stay in the depression – it doesn't feel good but it seems safer than the unknown step of what could be. We may not believe it can be better. Sometimes we hold on to anger and resentment because we think the wounds and the hurt are proof that we're right, that we've been done wrong, and it emboldens us in our distorted sense of justice. We choose to be miserable and "right" rather than experience healing and redemption. Paul chose to be comforted. He was rejuvenated by the words of support and hope from fellow believers. His identity was not defined by his circumstances but by his relationship with Christ.

Praise the God and Father of our Lord

Jesus Christ, the Father of mercies and the God of all comfort. He comforts us in all our affliction, so that we may be able to comfort those who are in any kind of affliction, through the comfort we ourselves receive from God. For as the sufferings of Christ overflow to us, so through Christ our comfort also overflows. If we are afflicted, it is for your comfort and salvation. If we are comforted, it is for your comfort, which is experienced in your endurance of the same sufferings that we suffer. And our hope for you is firm, because we know that as you share in the sufferings, so you will share in the comfort.
(2 Cor 1:3-7 HCSB)

Paul explained that we are comforted so that we can comfort others who are struggling or hurting. The peace and strength that we find in Him is the hope we can share with others. It doesn't mean we have all of the answers and can wave our magic wand but we know who holds the answers. We know the source of our strength. He's the "God of all comfort". His ability to comfort us is not based on the circumstances but on His character. He longs to comfort us, He equips and sends others to comfort us in our time of need. He also wants to use us in those times for others. Our ability to comfort others is not in having all of the right words. Spend time in prayer for those you know are hurting or feeling overwhelmed. Ask the Lord to bring to mind those you can reach out to.

Therefore comfort each other

and edify one another,

just as you also are doing.
(1 Thessalonians 5:11 NKJV)

Sometimes we forget or lose confidence in those who are there to support us as we go through difficult times. If you're struggling with depression, fear, hurt, betrayal, or overwhelming stress, allow others to comfort you. Be aware of being so insulated or isolated that others can't get through. It's ok if you initiate and reach out to others and let them know about your pain or struggle.

After my wife was diagnosed with cancer and was going in for surgery, Edwin was my Titus. He took time off work, drove down four hours from Atlanta, spent a few hours with me as we waited to hear the prognosis, and then drove four hours back home. We were old college friends, had been in bands together, were in each other's weddings, had been roommates in Statesboro, Savannah, and Atlanta, but hadn't seen each other in a while. Without hesitation, he was there to be support and encouragement. He brought a smile and laughter and was just there. There were many others who were an encouragement through that time and many others have played that role in my life over the years.

Take the time to remember who has been your Titus in your time of need. Don't let anger, resentment, depression, or your current situation overshadow those times when God ministered to you through others. Let it be an encouragement to you, that you are loved and cared for. We also have the opportunity to be Titus to someone who is hurting. Look around your social circles and identify who may need a hug, an encouraging note, or someone just to be with them.

Father, You are the God of all comfort. You sent Your Spirit, the comforter, to live in me. Help me to hear words of hope and encouragement. Help me to allow others to see the wounds and the struggle and for me to accept their help. Help me to comfort others with the same comfort I have experienced.

A Word of Hope for Today: He wants to comfort you. He will give you peace and calmness and strength, even when you don't expect it. He may also comfort you through others. If you are already being comforted by others, great! Keep on. If you're not, spend time with others and allow them to comfort you. Be encouraged by their words. Don't set them up for failure by expecting them to do this perfectly, but allow them to minister to you, pray for you, or prepare meals for you, if you need it. Your Heavenly Father designed you to live in community, this is not a weakness or a lack of faith, it's part of our design.

Comfort others. Encourage. Be patient. Be supportive. Be a friend. Listen. Trust Him to give you the words and the compassion.

Make a list of those in your community or social circle who may need comfort and care. Write a note. Make a visit. Send a message. Share a cup of coffee

Day 13

" Comfort, comfort My people," says your God.

Isaiah 40:1 (HCSB)

When we're wandering through the wilderness or the desert, we're usually looking for the quickest route out. But He may have a different plan in mind. His plan may not be just to help us escape the barren desert land but to walk with us through it. This is not what we want to hear. We want to hear it will be over. Soon. And then we'll get back to our real lives. But this route may not be the detour - this may be the journey He has allowed because He has a different plan in mind for us.

This is what the Lord says: "When seventy years are completed for Babylon, I will come to you and fulfill my good promise to bring you back to this place. For I know the plans I have for you," declares the Lord, "plans to prosper you and not to harm you, plans to give you hope and a future. Then you will call on me and come and pray to me, and I will listen to you. You will seek me and find me when you seek me with all your heart. I will be found by you," declares the Lord, "and will bring you back from captivity. I will gather you from all the nations and *places where I have banished you," declares the Lord, "and will bring you back to the place from which I carried you into exile."* (Jeremiah 29:10-14 NIV)

Sometimes we find ourselves in the wilderness because we make bad choices, we sin, we go our own way rather than His way. Sometimes it just happens - we live in a fallen world where death, decay, destruction, distractions, and captivity are a part of life. It's a part of the grind we go through. This doesn't mean He won't get us through it. We will make it through this - it may take time but we will make it through. And when we make it through - we will not be the same, we'll be transformed not just because of the journey but in Him. People go through difficult times and grow stronger. We toughen up. His work in us is bigger than just being stronger people, it is a work of holiness. His comfort is more than just making us feel better for a moment.

"Comfort, comfort My people," says your God. "Speak tenderly to Jerusalem, and announce to her that her time of forced labor is over, her iniquity has been pardoned, and she has received from the Lord's hand double for all her sins. "A voice of one crying out: Prepare the way of the Lord in the wilderness; make a straight highway for our God in the desert. Every valley will be lifted up, and every mountain and hill will be leveled;

the uneven ground will become smooth and the rough places, a plain. And the glory of the Lord will appear, and all humanity together will see [it], for the mouth of the Lord has spoken. (Isaiah 40:1-5 HCSB)

It can be hard to find peace in the desert because we want something different. We don't want to be in the desert so why would we want to find peace in the desert? We feel miserable, depressed, defeated, or overwhelmed and when it has been like this for months or years, we just want it to stop. But I can learn to be content here in the middle of this.

Contentment doesn't mean we just accept or settle for what is happening. It doesn't mean we give up on moving past this. It doesn't mean we plaster on the fake Christian smile and tell everyone we feel wonderful when we don't. It does mean we know where our help comes from. We know who our source of life is. We put our hope and faith and trust in the One who protects our soul. We believe He knows better than we do and we trust in His character. It doesn't mean we don't have days that are difficult - it is because we have these difficult days that we look to put our hope in something bigger than ourselves. It is holding on to the belief that His plans are to build us up not tear us down, that it is for our good even when it doesn't feel good, that His plans are to grow us rather than harm us. It is the peace that goes beyond our understanding, the peace that He can and will be with us through every step. It is the peace that is there in spite of the circumstances and emotions that are working against us. It is right here, right now believing He is with us and is working in us.

But the car won't start. I can't get out of bed. I'm too afraid. It's just too hard. It's too much. I'm overwhelmed. I can't make the money appear out of nowhere. It hurts so bad. They don't believe me, they don't understand. No one cares if I live or die. It's not right. It's not fair. I just feel empty. What's the point. There is no point. No one will help me. You don't know what he's like. She hurt me too bad. I feel dead inside. I don't feel anything inside. I don't care anymore. I already gave up. Those are the voices working against us. Can we believe, right here, right now, He is with us and is working in us? It may not work out the way we want it to. Can we let that dream die? Can we dream another dream? Can we believe He is alive and at work in us? We are the desert. He wants to do more than just make us feel better. He is bringing life and hope and water. He wants to do more than just take us from one place to another. He wants to take us from death to life.

It is difficult to believe this dark depression and overwhelming anxiety are what He means by abundant life. This can't be His holy, divine plan for us. Especially for believers, shouldn't His power and His Spirit in us result in more? But the depression, fear, and worry do not define us or define Him. And we shouldn't let it. The goal is not to just get rid of the depression and then we'll be happy. It is to experience life in Him regardless of the struggles and storms we are going through. The depression is exceedingly unpleasant and stifling. Our agenda may be to move on past it. His plan is for us to experience Him. He may be using these dark days for that purpose.

Our agenda may be to move on past it...
His plan is for us to experience Him.

More than just a quick pass to the front of the line, He gives me Him. When I'm honest, that's the part I struggle with. God, I choose immunity from trials rather than You and Your presence. Just chase the storm away then I'll feel better and will really worship You. I don't want You; I just want what You can do for me. Aren't You here to make me happy? Don't I get my three wishes? Can I be content with You? At Peace?

I love those days when it's storming outside and my wife and I lay around and are just lazy together. It doesn't matter how bad the wind is blowing or where the lightening is flashing, we're content just being together. *Heavenly Father, help me to be that content with You. Help me to be more focused on You and Your presence than on what is going on around me or in me. It's not that these concerns don't matter at all but You are greater than anything I am going through.* "If God is for us who is against us?" (Rom 8:31 HCSB). *You long to comfort Your people.*

He gives strength to the weary
and strengthens the powerless.
(Isaiah 40:29 HCSB)

He longs to comfort His people. Because we are struggling does not mean He does not care. If we only set our eyes on not feeling pain, we will miss

Him. That's me trying to comfort me. Can we allow Him to comfort us through the heartache and tragedy, through the loneliness and the hurt, through the stress and fear and doubt, through the long dark nights that seem endless?

God I don't know how to do this, help me...

Look up and see: who created these? He brings out the starry host by number; He calls all of them by name. Because of His great power and strength, not one of them is missing. Jacob, why do you say, and Israel, why do you assert: "My way is hidden from the Lord, and my claim is ignored by my God"? Do you not know? Have you not heard? Yahweh is the everlasting God, the Creator of the whole earth. He never grows faint or weary; there is no limit to His understanding. He gives strength to the weary and strengthens the powerless. Youths may faint and grow weary, and young men stumble and fall, but those who trust in the Lord will renew their strength; they will soar on wings like eagles; they will run and not grow weary; they will walk and not faint.

(Isaiah 40:26-31 HCSB)

Day 14

" And now, Lord, please take my life from me, for it is better for me to die than to live." The Lord asked, " Is it right for you to be angry?"
                                    Jonah 4:3,4 (HCSB)

Just a few days before this he was in the belly of a great fish crying out for help. He feared for his life. It's amazing what life inside a fish will do to motivate change. And now he was on a hillside overlooking Nineveh, wishing for death. The worm ate his shade plant and God had the audacity to make him this uncomfortable. Jonah was angry with God. Who was God to think He could make such flippant decisions without first consulting Jonah?

Jonah left the city and sat down east of it. He made himself a shelter there and sat in its shade to see what would happen to the city. Then the Lord God appointed a plant, and it grew up to provide shade over Jonah's head to ease his discomfort. Jonah was greatly pleased with the plant. When dawn came the next day, God appointed a worm that attacked the plant, and it withered. As the sun was rising, God appointed a scorching east wind. The sun beat down so much on Jonah's head that he almost fainted, and he wanted to die. He said, "It's better for me to die than to live. Then God asked Jonah, "Is it right for you to be angry about the plant?" "Yes," he replied. "It is right. I'm angry enough to die!"   (Jonah 4:5-9 HCSB)

God threw it back on Jonah, "Is it right for you to be so angry?" (v. 4). God asked the question twice. Jonah responded that he was justified in being this angry and he wanted God to know he was so angry he wished he was dead (v. 9). He didn't hold back. He let God know he was miserable and it was God's fault. How dare God show compassion and mercy on the Ninevites. Jonah was doing just fine sitting at home in his La-Z-Boy watching the game when God so rudely interrupted. He knew God wasn't going to go through with the whole destruction and desolation thing.   Why should Jonah's life be disrupted over all of this? He was angry because God is "a merciful and compassionate God, slow to become angry, rich in faithful love, and One who relents from [sending] disaster." (v. 2).

Jonah was angry because he knew God to be a God of compassion. This was the same compassion and mercy he cried out for in his time of need. God heard him even while Jonah was inside the great fish and God showed compassion.

He prayed to the Lord:
"Please, Lord, isn't this what I said while I was still in my own country?"
(Jonah 4:2 HCSB)

Jonah knew God's compassion. We first read

about Jonah in 2 Kings - during the corrupt reign of Jeroboam, God spoke "through His servant, the prophet Jonah son of Amittai from Gath-hepher." (2 Kings 14:25 HCSB). Jonah brought God's message of deliverance and salvation to Israel. It may have been the simple fact that God was pronouncing destruction on Nineveh but Jonah knew God to be compassionate and full of mercy. Nineveh was the capital of Assyria, which was often at war with Israel. Through the years, they had taken Israel into captivity. Why would Jonah want to go and warn the Ninevites? He explained he was opposed to the trip even before he left his "own country" (v. 4:2). His problem was not that God was compassionate but that God was compassionate to his enemies. He was all for mercy and compassion when it benefitted him.

We put ourselves on the throne when we want to decide who is shown mercy and who is not. Can we let God show mercy where He chooses to show mercy? Can we let Him sit on the throne? Can we honor and submit to His will rather than pushing ours? Can we be honest with ourselves about what we consider to be wrong or unjust? God blesses those we may not agree with or are unhappy with. Some of the "battles" we hold on to are not worth fighting. It's ok to forgive, we're called to forgive, to love others, to be compassionate. Sometimes we hold on to our sense of justice or "right-ness" so strongly that we get stuck. Sometimes we think others have to answer to us and repent before us rather than answering to their Heavenly Father. Is there an area of un-forgiveness or resentment that you have been holding on to? Is there someone you haven't forgiven because they are not doing what you think they are supposed to do? We can let those roots of bitterness grab a foothold and turn into strongholds. Jonah tried to justify himself before God but God called him on it.

"Are you right to be angry?" Jonah shot back an emphatic "Yes!" He cared more about his sense of rightness than God's. He cared more about the plant he had done nothing to create than the people he wished destruction upon. All of the emotion welling up inside of him did not make him right but he felt it passionately. He wasn't willing to show the compassion that had been shown to him in such an incredible way.

> " I knew that You are a merciful
> and compassionate God,
> slow to become angry, rich in
> faithful love, and One who relents
> from sending disaster."
> (Jonah 4:2b HCSB)

The great fish wasn't punishment; it was the means of salvation for Jonah. It also wasn't pleasant. It was a miserable life-or-death experience and he survived. God used the fish to put him where he needed to be. We usually look for the limo to pull up outside the door but God uses big fish, talking donkeys, stubborn mother-in-laws, difficult children, demanding bosses, overwhelming situations, or empty bank accounts. We see it as disruptions or failures but He sees it as an opportunity to shape and mold us. Jonah may have been grateful for the fish experience; we don't hear this in scripture but he may have told incredible accounts of it and testified how God rescued him from the great fish and from his selfish running. We don't hear it in scripture. Instead we see a man struggling with real life obstacles and powerful emotions. He let his anger and self-centeredness lead him astray. God met him on the ship as he ran, met him in the fish as he called out, met him in the city as he delivered the message, and met him outside the city where he was filled with self-pity.

Is there an area of your life that you're holding on to? Something that keeps you trapped more than the person you are holding it against? Has un-forgiveness, bitterness, or rage stolen your joy or peace? Is there a wound or pain that won't heal because you keep picking it open? Do you have to hold on to those wounds to prove others did you wrong? Do you keep replaying and reinforcing those thoughts or events to keep you wounded? Whether you feel stuck in the belly of a terrifying fish or you're sitting in the wasteland waiting for destruction to fall on your enemies, you can choose to let go of your sense of what should be. Jonah knew God to be a God of compassion and mercy. That was part of his anger. That was also his hope and deliverance. God wants to comfort you and bind up those wounds. Share your heart, your hurt, your anger, your tears. Let him be the God of comfort to your wounded-ness.

Father, You are my hope, my joy, my peace. Help me to be content in You. Help me to see the fish for what it is and be thankful. Help me to be obedient to what You are calling me to. I pray that I don't get in the way of what You're doing in my life or the lives of those around me. I want to be faithful. I want to live without fears or regrets. I want to put down my agenda and face those things that You are drawing my attention to. Help me to forgive and let go of those things that have hurt me in the past. I don't want it to define who I am. I choose to praise You through the good and the bad. I know that You are faithful and worthy of praise.

A Word of Hope for Today: Your life has purpose and meaning. You are valued by your Heavenly Father. Your circumstances may feel devestating and you don't believe there is a way out. He wants to see you through this.

If you are feeling overwhelmed or defeated and have thoughts of dying or self-harm, seek out a trusted pastor, friend, or counselor. Tell someone. Take a step to get help. Don't go through this alone. Don't keep it a secret. Call your local law enforcement, Emergency Room, or 911. There is no shame in getting help.

Day 15

Indeed, we have all received grace after grace from His fullness

John 1:16 (HCSB)

It's good to know we don't have to do this all on our own. "From His fullness.." - we are equipped and empowered out of His fullness, filled to fullness by Him. Filled to the brim.

Our lives may not always reflect that fullness but that is because of us, not Him. If He is who He says He is, we can trust Him to do what He said He would do. If He's not, then our hope is wasted anyway. Rather than trying to make Him into what we want Him to be, which would be a flawed, distorted image of Him, we can trust fully in Him to be who He is. We can allow Him to take us from death to life, from darkness to light.

Life was in Him,

and that life was the light of men.

That light shines in the darkness,

yet the darkness did not overcome it.

(John 1:4,5 HCSB)

There is a lot hidden in the darkness. Sin flourishes in the darkness. Depression and fear feed in the darkness. Anxiety, doubt, and dread cling to the darkness, it's how they stay alive. They breed all of the wrong answers and we often don't catch it because it all happens in the dark. We fall for it and believe the lies. The lies become the new "truth" we live by.

When the light shines in the darkness, it exposes the truth from the lies. *The darkness did not overcome the light*. We read in John chapter one that light came into the darkness, into the world. The world did not know Him, His own people did not receive Him (v. 10, 11). They fell for the lie that He was not God, that He could not save them, that they had to save themselves. But to those that do believe, "...He gave them the right to be children of God" (v. 12). Luke 1:79 tells us He came "to shine on those who live in darkness and the shadow of death, to guide our feet into the way of peace."(HCSB) In John we hear, "I have come as a light into the world, so that everyone who believes in Me would not remain in darkness." (John 12:46 HCSB)

Name your darkness. Is it fear, depression, anger, unbelief, hopelessness, worry, doubt, or grief? What keeps you thinking, feeling, or doing the same old things? Have you given up hope that things can be better? Have you fallen for the lies that you don't matter, God doesn't care, nothing can change, or that you are beyond His reach?

Let His light expose the lies and the darkness. "The Word became flesh and took up residence among us. We observed His glory, the glory as the One and Only Son from the Father, full of grace and truth." (John 1:14 HCSB) As He comes to live in us, we need to accept His truth - about Him, about us, about what forgiveness really means, about what real love is and how it transforms us, about sin and how it destroys us. We need to hear His truth and use it to challenge those thoughts that keep us living in fear and resentment and insecurity. Our understanding of truth needs to be defined by Him rather than by us, our experiences, or by our fluctuating emotions.

Since we have been rescued from our enemies' clutches, to serve Him without fear
(Luke 1:74 HCSB).

"Indeed, we have all received grace after grace from His fullness." From His fullness, we have received "grace after grace" - His favor. He chooses to shine His favor on us. We haven't earned it and don't deserve it, He gives it to us freely. Grace after grace, grace upon grace, we may not be aware of His favor on us. If we stay focused on our wants, desires, or discomforts, we may miss or overlook His favor for us. His truth says that He favors us, that He calls us His children: "But to all who did receive Him, He gave them the right to be children of God, to those who believe in His name." (John 1:12) "Look at how great a love the Father has given us that we should be called God's children. And we are! The reason the world does not know us is that it didn't know Him." (1 John 3:1 HCSB) Accepting His favor is accepting His truth that we need a Savior, that we are in darkness and in the shadow of death, that Jesus died for us, that His forgiveness is real, that His Spirit lives in us, that He loves us with an everlasting love. The darkness contradicts all of these truths. But His truth and light and life overcome the darkness.

What we read in John chapter one is more than

just someone getting a fresh start or starting a "new chapter" in their life. It is an Eternal God coming into a fallen, dark world. It is the point where God intervenes in an incredible way to bring salvation and deliverance. It is taking us from darkness to light, from death to life. It sounds a little dramatic. But it is that dramatic. It is the definition of drama – the original story. It is the development of the plot, the life or death situation: the tension has built, the problem has been identified, the tension is resolved as the hero steps in and "saves" the day. Only this story is not resolved in an hour-long episode. Jesus did not come into the world and die on a cross so we would go to church on Sunday morning. He came to reconcile us to God the Father, to give us life and hope and peace, to pay the penalty for our sin, to allow us overcome the power of sin and death in our lives. These are the things we can experience even in the midst of the desert, in the middle of the storm, in the darkest part of night.

> *For the Law was given*
> *through Moses;*
> *grace and truth were*
> *realized through Jesus Christ.*
> (John 1:17 NASB)

When our faith is just something we do on Sunday mornings or just thinking we are good, deserving people, we miss the power of what it means to go from death to life, darkness to light. Can we experience "grace after grace from His fullness" in our everyday chaotic lives? Can we experience it when every day seems to be drudgery just to get up and get going, when the tears won't seem to stop, when the overwhelming black hole of depression or despair consumes every minute and every thought? When we exchange our lies for His truth, we understand that our hope is not that He will make it all just go away.

Jesus did not come just to make us feel better or to make us happy and grant every wish. He came to give us life and hope. He came to transform us. What beliefs are keeping you from that today? Bring those to the Lord in prayer. Believe He is with you through whatever you are facing today.

Don't worry about anything,
but in everything,
through prayer and petition
with thanksgiving,
let your requests be made known to God.
And the peace of God,
which surpasses every thought,
will guard your hearts and minds
in Christ Jesus.
(Philippians 4:6,7 HCSB)

Today, I can trust in You for the fullness of all that I need. Help me to walk in the light as You are in the light. Help me to know Your truth and live like it's true.

A Word of Hope for Today: He will be with you through the darkest of days. That is our hope. He came into the world to be with you, to connect with you, to reconcile you back to Him. He will not leave you or forsake you. He is your God, you are His child, He is with you.

Take the time to write out what you are telling yourself. Be honest and vulnerable. Write out (word for word) your thoughts about life, God, you, your situation, your fears. Compare and contrast these with God's truth. Challenge the thoughts that are grounded in fear and doubt, tainted by unstable emotions, or riddled with self-defeat.

For though we live in the body, we do not wage war in an unspiritual way, since the weapons of our warfare are not worldly, but are powerful through God for the demolition of strongholds. We demolish arguments and every high-minded thing that is raised up against the knowledge of God, taking every thought captive to obey Christ.

2 Corinthians 10:3 - 5

Vines Expository Dictionary of New Testament Words explains "stronghold" as a metaphor for "those things in which mere human confidence is imposed." It is a stronghold, a fortress, something we have built up to defend or enforce a perspective. It is those in which we, intentionally or unintentionally, put our faith or hope. They are our core beliefs about where we find our strength and security.

Paul clearly defined the battle as spiritual - "we do not wage war in an unspiritual way, since the weapons of our warfare are not worldly, but are powerful through God..." He described it as a battle of arguments and thoughts waging war against the knowledge of God. The NIV words it as "...arguments and every pretension that sets itself up against the knowledge of God, and we take captive every thought..." (v. 5). Webster's defines pretense as "a false reason or explanation that is used to hide the real purpose of something." The NASB uses the word "speculations". The New Living Translation says, "the strongholds of human reasoning and... false arguments." It is a battle of thoughts, theories, and conjectures in the mind. Paul instructs us to bring every thought captive in obedience to Christ. When we put our confidence and hope, in the ways of the world or worldly wisdom, we set ourselves opposed to the ways of God. These are in direct opposition to each other.

> ... for the weapons of our warfare
> are not of the flesh,
> but divinely powerful
> for the destruction of fortresses.
> (2 Cor. 10:4 NASB)

I like that Paul says our spiritual weapons "are powerful through God for the *demolition* of strongholds. We *demolish* arguments." (v.4) In Him and with Him in us, we can destroy the opposition. We can overcome the thoughts and speculations that wage war against us. We can defeat the enemy and his schemes that come against us, that undermine us and deflate us. It is that enemy that steals our joy and tries to crush our hope. He pulls the rug out from underneath us, leaving us with no foundation. But, in Christ, we can be victorious.

> Why, my soul, are you downcast?
> Why so disturbed within me?
> Put your hope in God,

for I will yet praise him,
my Savior and my God.
(Psalm 42:5)

You may already feel weary and defeated. You may feel overwhelmed and empty, dried-out and cast aside. That is part of the enemy's strategy - to get us to believe it will not get better; to make us think we are all alone; to say to ourselves there is no hope; to get us to stop praying. We stop turning to God for help.

Satan's goal is not to get us to worship him, it is to get us to not worship our Heavenly Father. He doesn't have to convince us that he is the solution, he just wants us to fall for the lie that we can solve it without God. Depression and anxiety feed into the pretense that God doesn't care. It becomes easier to live defeated and stop believing God is with us. Paul tells us something different. The word of God tells us our weapons demolish arguments and thoughts that are out of line with God's reality.

Finally, be strong in the Lord
and in the strength of His might.
(Eph. 6:10 NASB)

What are these weapons? Ephesians 6 describes "the armor of God" which includes the Sword of the Spirit - His Word, the Bible is one of our main weapons, it is His truth. It is more than just a historical account, it is truth about us, life, God, and His far-reaching love for us. It is truth that challenges the world's wisdom or human reason. If we're going to defeat and demolish the arguments and thoughts working against us, we need to know His truth about us.

His Spirit, alive and living in us is a powerful weapon. Do our lives look different because an Almighty God dwells inside each one of us? Our lives should look different. How we decide and what we decide should be different than worldly wisdom. Jesus came to save us and reconcile us to the Father. He said He was sending a helper, a comforter and counselor, the Holy Spirit, to live in us and to empower us to live the lives He has set us free to live. His strength, His power is Him living in us. As Paul was writing to the Church about being equipped with armor he introduced the idea with this perspective, "Finally, be strong in the Lord and in his mighty power." (Eph. 6:10 NIV) we are to find our strength in His strength.

with this in mind, be alert,

and keep on praying...
(Ephesians 6:18)

Paul described the armor: the Word of God, our salvation and security, truth, our righteousness in Him, the Gospel of peace, and our faith. He then encouraged believers to "pray in the Spirit on all occasions with all kinds of prayers and requests. With this in mind, be alert and always keep on praying for all the Lord's people." (Eph. 6:18 NIV) Prayer is a powerful weapon at our disposal. It means we are not alone in this. Not only is His Spirit on us to empower and equip us, His Spirit helps us to pray and stay connected with our Heavenly Father. It almost sounds like He is setting us up to win, He wants us to succeed. He warns us, "with this in mind, be alert, and keep on praying..." Be aware of your thoughts, be attentive - you are in a battle zone but don't lose contact with Him.

Other weapons we have are love, forgiveness, mercy, wisdom, and hope. We demolish the attacks of the enemy when we practice these. Other people are not "the enemy". We may struggle or feel attacked and wounded by others but real love and forgiveness work through this in a way that God is glorified, we are transformed, and others are impacted. Worldly wisdom may tell you to look out for yourself, make others pay for what they do, or find your security in money, material things, or accomplishments. But our weapons are not of the flesh. It may not make sense to forgive that person who wounded you deeply but you will not be tied up in hatred, resentment, or the past. Serving others may seem like a punishment or you're being taken advantage of but you know it is your choice to serve. Others may not understand why you're not driven to store up material possessions but you'll know the things you own don't own you. What the world defines as wealth or success, God defines as bondage. When we start to pile up toys, the flesh has to find worldly ways to keep them. We fear losing possessions, opportunities, or prestige. These turn into strongholds.

...and after you have done everything,

to stand. Stand firm then

(Ephesians 6:13b, 14a)

Father, You said You would guard my heart and my mind. Help me to be aware of how often my own thoughts work against me. Help me to find my strength in You, to take Your word as truth, to trust in the work You are doing in me. Help me to recognize and challenge the thoughts, ideas, perceptions, patterns, and methods that are not of You.

A Word of Hope for Today: Is there a war raging inside of you? Is your mind under attack? Use His word, His truth, to challenge the arguments and speculations contrary to God's reality. Are there strongholds built up because of bitterness, unforgiveness, or past wounds? Worldly justice would tell you to hold on to these. Your Heavenly Father encourages you to forgive and love but also to be healed of these. Are there strongholds in patterns of broken relationships and an unwillingness to trust others? Is there a stronghold of finding value, meaning, or security in material possessions or your checkbook? Do you struggle to take down the fortress walls that keep you safe but insulated or isolated?

Name the walls, the defenses that you put up or keep in place to protect you. Exchange your weapons for His.

Day 17

Above all, love each other deeply, because love covers over a multitude of sins.

(1 Peter 4:8 NIV)

Most of all, love each other as if your life depended on it. Love makes up for practically anything.

(1 Peter 4:8 The Message)

Now that you have purified yourselves by obeying the truth so that you have sincere love for each other, love one another deeply, from the heart. (1 Peter 1:22 NIV)

My command is this: Love each other as I have loved you. Greater love has no one than this: to lay down one's life for one's friends. (John 15:12, 13 NIV)

Healthy relationships. Eugene Peterson translated "love one another deeply" as "love others as if your life depended on it." What if a full, meaningful life does depend on it? What if moving through the guilt, depression, resentment, or anxiety requires genuinely staying connected to others? What if what God wants to heal or fulfill in us is going to happen as we continue to engage in the lives of others?

"A new command I give you:
Love one another.
As I have loved you,
so you must love one another."
(John 13:34 NIV)

We're told repeatedly in scripture to love others. Jesus commanded, "Love each other as I have loved you." (John 15:12 NIV) His life depended on it. That was "loving deeply". He took the call to love others seriously. If we take His words seriously, we will love others in a meaningful way - in a way that is transformational for them and for us. It is a love that comes with a cost, a love that gives, a love that has in mind what is ultimately good for others rather than just what feels good to us for the moment. It is other-focused. Sometimes it feels like it would be easier to walk on water than to love others. Other-focused means we can be distracted from focusing so much on ourselves and our circumstances. Anxiety is often focused on ourselves or others in an unhealthy way. Instead of focusing on what is good, lovely, and upright, it can consume us with fear, doubt, and skepticism. It's difficult to reach out to others when we're feeling all of that. It drains us. Our eyes can get focused on worldly problems and worldly solutions; oblivious to the kingdom around us and His Spirit within us.

Depression has a way of isolating us from others. We pull away, shut down emotionally, or just avoid. It becomes easier to disengage and it takes a lot less energy. It's difficult to genuinely invest in others when depression takes over and steals our joy, our hope, and our strength. It feels overwhelming to deal with our own issues, let alone tying to be empathetic to some one else's set of problems. And, disconnecting from others perpetuates the negative patterns. It feels good initially and we may avoid some uncomfortable feelings but it reinforces the self-feeding patterns of depression and anxiety. What feels good for the moment digs the hole deeper.

*Be good friends who love deeply;
practice playing second fiddle.*
(Romans 12:10 The Message)

Depression and worries are not the reason to avoid others but the reason to embrace them. Especially, those who are hurting just like we are. We can comfort others because of the comfort we have received. We can understand the hurt and pain of some that feel alone and misunderstood. Loving others may be so vital because what God is calling us to is more than just being polite. Rick Rigsby said that we're not called to just make a nice impression on others but to have an impact on them. Loving others deeply takes me out of my comfort zone. I try hard to be polite and not offend others. The problem is I can be a nice person and still stay disconnected. I can be friendly and never really get to know anyone. Or, be known by anyone. No intrusion but also no impact. Jesus calls us to actively and intentionally love others: to love in the same way He loved. To love as if our lives depended on it. His Spirit is at work in us as we live genuinely in community with others.

Beloved, if God so loved us,
we also ought to love one another.
(1 John 4:11)

Loving others also gives others an opportunity to love us in return. If we'll accept it. We can allow ourselves to truly be vulnerable. Allowing others to see our weaknesses does not take away from God's power or glory. Paul knew this, *"and He has said to me, 'My grace is sufficient for you, for power is perfected in weakness.' Most gladly, therefore, I will rather boast about my weaknesses, so that the power of Christ may dwell in me. Therefore I am well content with weaknesses, with insults, with distresses, with persecutions, with difficulties, for Christ's sake; for when I am weak, then I am strong."* (2 Corinthians 12:9,10 NASB)

There is a healing and fullness that comes as we live connected to the Body of Christ, as we have to work through conflict, anger, or hurt feelings, as we choose to live out what our Heavenly Father is calling us to. We can experience what it means to be connected to others in the Body when we hurt as they hurt and grieve as they grieve. We experience it when we speak the truth in love and respond to their defensiveness with more love, when we come along side and encourage the one who feels they cannot take another step and they're not even sure there is another step to take. John states very clearly, *"The one who does not love does not know God, for God is love."* (1 John 4:8 NASB) Jesus told us how important it is to love others – He put it second after loving God with our whole heart: "love your neighbor as yourself." We get these commandments wrong - we get it backwards when we start with loving ourselves. When we put ourselves on the throne.

"The most important one," answered Jesus, "is this: 'Hear, O Israel: The Lord our God, the Lord is one. Love the Lord your God with all your heart and with all your soul and with all your mind and with all your strength.' The second is this: 'Love your neighbor as yourself.' There is no commandment greater than these."

(Mark 12:29-31 NIV)

Father, You know the walls I put up to keep me safe. You know when I genuinely reach out to others and when I am just going through the motions. Help me to love others deeply, often, genuinely. Help me to see others for who they are – people You love and sent Your son to die for. You love us that deeply. Show me through out the day and the rest of the week those who are hurting, those who need encouragement, and those who are struggling with doubt, shame, fear, rejection, hurt, depression, and feeling unloved.

A Word of Hope for Today: God loves you. He sent His Son to die for you. We love because He first loved us (1 Jn 4:19) God will use those around you to connect and encourage you. Be open to it. Be intentional to connect with them in a meaningful way. Look around to see who you can reach out to. Often, that ministers to us as well as to them – it takes the focus off of us, our problems, or what we are going through. Sometimes, it just gives us perspective that what we are going through may not be as bad as what others are facing. God uses these intentional, meaningful relationships to help us face what we often want to hide. Rather than addressing these issues alone and in the dark, He opens up opportunities to deal with it in the light with others around us to help encourage and challenge and lift us up.

The Lord is my shepherd; I shall not want. He maketh me to lie down in green pastures: he leadeth me beside the still waters. He restoreth my soul: he leadeth me in the paths of righteousness for his name's sake. Yea, though I walk through the valley of the shadow of death, I will fear no evil: for thou art with me; thy rod and thy staff they comfort me. Thou preparest a table before me in the presence of mine enemies: thou anointest my head with oil; my cup runneth over. Surely goodness and mercy shall follow me all the days of my life: and I will dwell in the house of the Lord forever.

Psalm 23:1-6 (KJV)

"He restores my soul." I need that. On those days when we're not really sure where we're going or what we're doing, we need to know we will be ok. When the walls are closing in and the storm is swelling outside, we can find comfort knowing we are secure.

David knew that comfort. There is a reason this psalm is quoted in the darkest of times. There is calmness and reassurance in David's words. There is a confidence and conviction - he knew who his shepherd was. "The Lord is my shepherd." The Lord God, Yahweh. David's confidence was in the character of his God. And he knew his God was sufficient, He is more than able to handle what ever comes up. This is why David could say he lacked nothing, he was in need of nothing, and he "shall not want". Sometimes we need to know, we need to hear again, we are safe in His arms.

This passage can also seem like a contradiction. If He leads us beside still waters and restores our souls then what is there to fear? If the Lord leads us in the paths of righteousness then why do we have to go through the valley of the shadow of death?

"The valley of the shadow of death" - it takes a person who genuinely knows those low times to come up with a description like that. We hear David's struggles and doubts throughout the Psalms. He didn't claim not to feel overwhelmed with emotion at times. We hear his confidence but also his moments of defeat. "I sink in the miry depths, where there is no foothold. I have come into the deep waters; the floods engulf me." (Psalm 69:2 NIV) But through it all, he knew who to trust, "Answer me when I call to you, my righteous God. Give me relief from my distress; have mercy on me and hear my prayer." (Psalm 4:1 NIV) Unfortunately, we have to go through the valleys.

I will fear no evil;
For You are with me
(v. 4 NKJV)

Those things that pressure us and overwhelm can also overshadow and distract us. It becomes easier to focus on the dark valleys rather than the pleasant streams. David's confidence was not in God's ability to make all of the bad things go away. It was confidence in God: "You are with me." This is our confidence and our peace. God was with him in the green pastures, beside the still waters, and along the paths of righteousness. But He was also there walking with him through the valley of the shadow of death and seated with him at the table surrounded by his enemies.

David understood all of this was the Lord God leading and guiding him along the paths of righteousness. Even if there was an ambush, his faithful guide was confident in the course. The Shepherd's ability to handle whatever crept in was David's confidence - "Thy rod and Thy staff they comfort me." We find our strength in the strength of His might (Eph. 6:10). We need to believe we can do all things through Christ who strengthens us (Phil. 4:12). David knew he didn't have to fear evil and made the choice not to - "I will fear no evil."

Surely goodness and mercy shall follow me all the days of my life.
(v. 6 NKJV)

David wrote with a sense of permanency, "Surely goodness and mercy shall follow me all the days of my life: and I will dwell in the house of the Lord for ever." That he could say goodness and mercy would follow him all the days of His life testified of his hope even through the darkest valleys. The Lord's goodness and mercy were not absent. In spite of what his emotions must have been telling him, he was never abandoned. "All the days" of his life, it didn't always feel like goodness or mercy but he could see he was never alone. Even through sinful choices, God dealt with him fairly and justly and with mercy.

When feelings of doubt and insecurity creep in, what are the thoughts associated with that? How often do your thoughts revert back to the intensity or severity of the situation or problem rather than the Lord's ability to overcome it? Is your first thought on how overwhelming the circumstances are or the assurance that, even in this, there is nothing to fear? He is with you; He restores and refreshes your soul. Pray through Psalm 23 again with the confidence and assurance that the Lord is your shepherd and you lack nothing.

The Lord is my shepherd; there is nothing I lack. He lets me lie down in green pastures; He leads me beside quiet waters. He renews my life; He leads me along the right paths for His name's sake. Even when I go through the darkest valley, I fear no danger, for You are with me; Your rod and Your staff—they comfort me. You prepare a table before me in the presence of my enemies; You anoint my head with oil; my cup overflows. Only goodness and faithful love will pursue me all the days of my life, and I will dwell in the house of the Lord as long as I live. Amen
(Psalm 23 HCSB)

A Word of Hope for Today: You are not alone. The dark valleys are not proof that He has left you or abandoned you. The dark valleys are not a sign that He does not care for you. His desire is to be with you through all that you are going through. He will be glorified and others will be impacted as you walk with Him through the midst of the shadows. His rod and His staff are His strength and power to see you through this. You will make it through this.

Day 19

And the peace of God, which surpasses all comprehension, will guard your hearts and your minds in Christ Jesus.

Philippians 4:7 (NASB)

Peace. Shalom. In Hebrew, shalom means peace, wholeness, complete. We often understand peace to be the absence of war or conflict. No hostility between the two parts. "Eirene" (gk) the greek word for peace comes from the primary verb "eiro" meaning "to join" (Blue Letter Bible). The two parts become one. That is that sense of wholeness, completeness, the pieces of the puzzle all fit together; there is no conflict between them. Todo bien. It's *all* good.

That is the peace that we have as believers. We don't always see how it will work out or fit together but we trust that He does. We can be at peace. *"And we know that God causes all things to work together for good to those who love God, to those who are called according to His purpose."* (Rom. 8:28 NASB) *"... by the exertion of the power that He has even to subject all things to Himself."* (Phil. 3:21b NASB)

Therefore, having been justified by faith,
we have peace with God
through our Lord Jesus Christ
(Romans 5:1 NASB)

Our peace is that we are one with Him, one in Him. Not divided, not separated from Him, in Him we are complete. The result of our faith is not just to make us "good" people but to reconcile us back to God, to make us whole, complete, holy. He is the God of peace. Our peace comes when we can turn it all over to Him, trusting we are safe in Him. *"Be anxious for nothing, but in everything by prayer and supplication with thanksgiving let your requests be made known to God. And the peace of God, which surpasses all comprehension, will guard your hearts and your minds in Christ Jesus."* (Philippians 4:6, 7 NASB)

We don't want the bad things that happen: the losses, the wounds, the rejections, the fears, and the struggles. God sees these and uses them for our good. We experience these and want to avoid them. We just want it to all go away. We have our own agenda to deal with these; an agenda different than His, which divides us. Peace means we are able to allow Him to be with us through these times and we trust His judgment rather than our own. Rather than trying to get Him to go along with my plans, can I submit to His? That's when we experience His peace. That's the peace that passes all understanding, all comprehension.

God, I don't want this and I don't want to hurt like this. I don't see the good in it and I don't understand it. I need Your peace to guard my heart and mind because my thoughts and emotions will take me in directions I don't need to go. Help me to trust You with all I am going through.

For the mind set on the flesh is death,
but the mind set on the Spirit
is life and peace,
because the mind set on the flesh
is hostile toward God; for it does not
subject itself to the law of God,
for it is not even able to do so,
(Romans 8:6,7 NASB)

Our part in the battle is believing and accepting to surrender to His lordship. We don't experience peace when we think we know better. But also when we don't like the way we feel – feeling depressed, overwhelmed, stressed, hurt, resentful, and defeated – it doesn't feel right to surrender more, unsure it will all work out. But so often, our emotions work against us. Jesus experienced that same feeling as He was preparing to face the cross. *"Taking along Peter and the two sons of Zebedee, He began to be sorrowful and deeply distressed. Then He said to them, 'My soul is swallowed up in sorrow —to the point of death. Remain here and stay awake with Me' Going a little farther, He fell facedown and prayed, 'My Father! If it is possible, let this cup pass from Me. Yet not as I will, but as You will.'"* (Mt. 26:37-39 HCSB) His initial response to the overwhelming situation was to ask His Father to make it all go away but He also knew His Father's will and submitted to that. The human side of Him was struggling, His peace came from being one with the Father, believing that even through this, His Father would be with Him and empower Him to do what He needed to do.

*Do what you have learned
and received and heard and seen in me,
and the God of peace will be with you.*
(Philippians 4:9 HCSB)

It will not improve anything to go on carrying the weight of all the stress or pain. When you're feeling overwhelmed with all of the "what ifs" and replaying over and over what was said or done, ask yourself is it helping you or hurting you? Worrying about it for 10 more minutes or 10 more days will not fix anything, it will only continue to tear you down. His peace will assure you it will be ok; our fears and worries and troublesome thoughts will twist our situations into the worst-case scenario.

"Don't worry about anything, but in everything, through prayer and petition with thanksgiving, let your requests be made known to God. And the peace of God, which surpasses every thought, will guard your hearts and minds in Christ Jesus. Finally brothers, whatever is true, whatever is honorable, whatever is just, whatever is pure, whatever is lovely, whatever is commendable— if there is any moral excellence and if there is any praise—dwell on these things. Do what you have learned and received and heard and seen in me, and the God of peace will be with you." (Philippians 4:6-9 HCSB)

Father, Help me to trust in You. So often, there is a war going on inside of me, I am not at peace and don't feel Your peace. I give all of my life up to You, the good and the bad. I trust You with everything. You know the hurt and pain, the daily struggles just to get up or get going, the open wounds that I carry around. I choose to trust You, knowing that You are more than able to handle all that I am going through, nothing has taken You by surprise. I want to experience Your peace, Your joy, Your strength in my life. Take this cup from me, but if You choose not to, "not as I will, but as You will." I know that You are with me through it all.

A Word of Hope for Today: Continue to turn everything over to Him. Hour by hour, moment by moment, bring *everything* to Him in prayer. When you are not experiencing His peace, ask yourself if it is because you are opposing His will. He may not choose to take it all away but He will be with you through it all. His promise is He will be with you. His purpose is for you to experience the peace of God and the God of peace.

"Remember that you were at that time separate from Christ, excluded from the commonwealth of Israel, and strangers to the covenants of promise, having no hope and without God in the world. But now in Christ Jesus you who formerly were far off have been brought near by the blood of Christ. For He Himself is our peace, who made both groups into one and broke down the barrier of the dividing wall, by abolishing in His flesh the enmity, which is the Law of commandments contained in ordinances, so that in Himself He might make the two into one new man, thus establishing peace." (Eph. 2:12-15 NASB)

Day 20

" Be strong and courageous, for you will distribute the land I swore to their fathers to give them as an inheritance. Above all, be strong and very courageous to carefully observe the whole instruction My servant Moses commanded you. Do not turn from it to the right or the left, so that you will have success wherever you go. This book of instruction must not depart from your mouth; you are to recite it day and night so that you may carefully observe everything written in it. For then you will prosper and succeed in whatever you do. Haven't I commanded you: be strong and courageous? Do not be afraid or discouraged, for the Lord your God is with you wherever you go."

Joshua 1:6-9 (HCSB)

Courage is not the absence of fear, it is action and attitude in spite of the fear. If we wait for the fear to go away before we step into action, we may be waiting a long time or we may not take a step. God instructed his servant, Joshua, to be strong and courageous, to press on in obedience and reliance on the Lord.

It takes courage to change. Change can be unknown and we're not always convinced the results or outcome of change will be worth the effort. What if we fail? Most of the time, we do what we do because it's comfortable.

Change is sometimes motivated by pain. When the pain of our current situation becomes unbearable, we change. If it is bearable, we stay right where we are. Even if we don't like the circumstances, there is a certain familiarity or comfort in staying where or how we currently are. We may not like it but at least we know what to expect. Sometimes desires or wants motivate change. We want more than we have now, we can see the benefit in doing more, being more, or being different. Others may encourage or demand change so they apply leverage to initiate the change.

We resist it. Usually, we react strongly to it when we first hear about it. Most of us think change is a bad thing. When your doctor says you have to change your diet or exercise routine, that's not usually a welcomed suggestion. It is different when the change is known to be good. If someone tells us we have just won 8 billion dollars, we don't usually frown on that. We may be skeptical but our minds go right to how this new change will benefit us.

A change was coming for Joshua and the people of Israel. They were about to cross into the Promised Land. It was what they were longing for but it also brought new challenges with it. It was a "land flowing with milk and honey" but also a land that had to be conquered. It was not sitting there empty waiting to be occupied.

Have you set up an idealized "promised land" in your mind? That place or state of being where it will all be perfect or easy or free from all distractions and hassles? Are you avoiding things now because you are waiting for a magical thing to happen that will make it all fall into place?

> *" No one will be able to stand against you all the days of your life. As I was with Moses, so I will be with you; I will never leave you nor forsake you."*
> (Joshua 1:5)

Joshua was instructed to be strong and courageous three times in verses 6 – 9. The Lord's instructions to Joshua were more than just wishful thinking or a mini pep rally. It was more than a moral value that He was passing on to Joshua. God explained why Joshua was to be courageous, "No one will be able to stand against you all the days of your life. As I was with Moses, so I will be with you; I will never leave you nor forsake you." (Joshua 1:5) It took courage to move forward. Even though the Lord was with the Israelites some of them did not make it to the Promised Land. Some fell at the hands of the enemy. But, the Lord was with them. Joshua's encouragement was the assurance that the Lord was with them, He would go before them, He would be their God in their midst. This was their confidence that what would come about would be according to His divine plan on the condition that they were faithful to walk with Him.

It takes courage to change. It takes strength to

intentionally step out and challenge the old patterns that are not working. We can challenge the old thoughts that produce the same old feelings which produce those same old behaviors. We have to be willing to step forward and believe that His word is truth rather than our misdirected or distorted perceptions. We have to rely on His strength when we don't want to get up out of the chair but we know that we need to. We need to rely on His Spirit to transform us as we step out in faith and do the work He is calling us to do. Don't wait for the feeling to change before you take a step. Don't believe what your feelings are telling you.

> For God has not given us
> a spirit of fear,
> but of power and of love
> and of a sound mind.
> (2 Timothy 1:7 NKJV)

Be honest about the fears that have impacted your life. Is there a fear of failure, a fear of not being loved, a fear of not being enough, a fear of being alone? Is there a fear of the unknown? Are you filling in too many blanks where you don't know the answers but you assume that you do? Is there a fear that others may see you for who you really are if they get too close? That's a scary place to be. You know your flaws, all of the unlovable parts of you. You know the ugly truth about who you are when no one is looking and the thoughts that no one else can hear.

Are you willing to let others get close? Vulnerability and transparency may be unsettling terms but it is what He is calling us to. Not everyone is safe enough to share our real selves with. Some people are toxic or hurtful or unhealthy; it may not be safe to open up with some. People hurt people. But not everyone is like that, regardless of what your fear may tell you. Some are safe. To be transparent and real with others may mean we have to trust more in God than in them. He is with us. He will not forsake us. He will be with us through whatever comes up.

To be strong and courageous may mean we dive in and invest in relationships. It's a land flowing with milk and honey but it also has obstacles that have to be overcome. Relationships are the same. Because we're human, we intentionally and unintentionally hurt one another. There is a risk but we also have a God who will go before us. This doesn't mean that we open ourselves up to the most un-healthy people we can find; it does mean that we go into relationships knowing there will be issues to work through. They will see our imperfections and we will see theirs.

There is no fear in love;

but perfect love casts out fear

(1 John 4:18a NKJV)

To be strong and courageous may mean that we are honest about those imperfections. We have to admit our flaws, our weaknesses, our sin. In the light they can be dealt with and addressed; in the dark they just stay hidden and do not heal. If conflict comes up, God will use these situations to teach us how to work through them and stay connected to one another.

" Is anyone among you suffering? He should pray. Is anyone cheerful? He should sing praises. Is anyone among you sick? He should call for the elders of the church, and they should pray over him after anointing him with olive oil in the name of the Lord. The prayer of faith will save the sick person, and the Lord will restore him to health; if he has committed sins, he will be forgiven. Therefore, confess your sins to one another and pray for one another, so that you may be healed. The urgent request of a righteous person is very powerful in its effect."

(James 5:13-16 HCSB)

Father, you know my heart. You know the insecurities that are there. You know the behavior I've learned or adapted to keep myself safe but it also keeps me isolated from others. You intend for us to live in community, to be Your body, Your gathering of people. Help me to be strong and courageous as I let the walls down. Help me to not turn to the right or to the left but to meditate day and night on Your word. Your words are truth and teach us how to love one another.

A Word of Hope for Today: Perfect love casts out fear. His love casts out fear. You are safe in His care. It may not always feel safe. Your thoughts may tell you to be afraid. Be honest about the fear that is there. To overcome fear, you have to be willing to be uncomfortable. Allow the anxiety to go up. Usually our behavior is designed to go back to normal, back to our comfort level, meaning we give in to the fear. To overcome the fear, you have to be willing to face what you are afraid of and be aware this will not feel pleasant. If it is a fear of failure, a fear of crowded spaces, a fear of being alone, a fear of not being perfect, face the fear. Take a step, be willing to do something fear has kept you from. Today.

Moreover, I will give you a new heart and put a new spirit within you; and I will remove the heart of stone from your flesh and give you a heart of flesh. I will put My Spirit within you and cause you to walk in My statutes, and you will be careful to observe My ordinances. You will live in the land that I gave to your forefathers; so you will be My people, and I will be your God.

Ezekiel 36:26-28 (NASB)

If God is who He says He is, then everything is about Him, He is the Center. He existed before time. He is eternal and forever will be. He spoke the words and everything we know came into being. Everything we know was created by Him and is defined by Him. Good and evil are determined in reference to Him. If He is who He says He is, then purpose and meaning are centered in Him. That's where our emotions come in and hijack the show.

Our emotions can be a demanding taskmaster. They have a way of making most things about us. Emotions are not evil. God has emotions. Created in His image, we were designed to experience feelings. Like anything else, if we are wholly submitted to Christ, our emotions are submitted to Christ. But even then, our emotions can get the best of us. If we're not living in submission to His reign, something else is controlling us and often that is our emotions, our own desires or pleasure. We like to feel good.

The heart is deceitful above all things and beyond cure. Who can understand it?
(Jeremiah 17:9 NIV)

We do what feels good to us. We avoid conflict. We act selfish. We criticize others. We tend to emotionally disconnect when it gets uncomfortable. We please others to make ourselves feel good. We sometimes become numb or indifferent because we would rather feel nothing than to feel bad.

Research in human development over the past years indicates that our brains are still developing into our mid 20's. Specifically, the part still developing is the frontal lobe, the part of the brain that has to do with logic or rational thought. This doesn't mean that we are not smart before then but it explains why people make so many irrational, emotion-drenched decisions. A lot happens in life as our brains are still "under construction" - moral development, future goals, establishing priorities, learning to navigate relationships, dating, courting, marriage, having children, setting a life direction, etc... Rational thought would help a lot when choosing the person you're going to spend the rest of your life with. The heart usually trumps all of the rational arguments.

I will give you a new heart and put a new spirit in you; I will remove from you your heart of stone and give you a heart of flesh.

(Ezekiel 36:26 NIV)

Even when the rational brain matures, we still may have those moments when emotional reasoning takes over. In his book, Emotional Intelligence, Daniel Goleman described this as an "emotional hijacking" when a fight or flight response is activated by a real or perceived threat. Emotion grabs the steering wheel because of fear, aggression, excitement, danger, or anger. In that moment, our thoughts and reactions are controlled by our emotions in self-protection mode. (1)

The problem is that not every reaction like that is response to a life-or-death situation. We may perceive danger or an attack on our person that is not there. That God-given defense mechanism that is supposed to kick in immediately when we're being chased by a grizzly bear shifts into high gear when we mistakenly take a joke too personally or have a disagreement with a spouse. Our emotional reaction in that moment is to win, to crush the "enemy", to dominate, to "protect" ourselves.

Sometimes, emotion may be driving the ship because we can't or don't want to say "no" to ourselves. We're unwilling to delay immediate gratification. We like feeling good and we're willing to pay the cost later... maybe.. but we probably won't *feel* like paying then either.

We do a lot of emotional reasoning. We come into the world wired this way. Babies cry to get what they want... And everybody comes running... Even at four in the morning. That's a lot of power. A lot of reinforcement that our emotional desires should all be met. Immediately. And, there's something seriously wrong with the world if we're unhappy or uncomfortable.

Our emotions rule us.

And then a new sheriff rides into town. And there isn't room for two kings on the throne. We surrender to Jesus and He gives us a new heart and renews our minds but those pesky emotions have a way of holding on and causing havoc. They are part of the old regime that goes underground and raises their ugly head any time they "feel" like it. And it feels good. It feels full. Emotions aren't all bad. They're powerful. God gave them to us for a reason. Excitement, passion, compassion, desire, awe, love, adoration, humility, overwhelmed, peace, joy, fulfillment, and wonder are all emotions we need to experience in His presence as we worship Him. He gave us emotions so we could experience Him in the fullest.

Delight yourself in the LORD;
And He will give you
the desires of your heart.
(Psalm 37:4 NASB)

When we delight in Him our hearts will be full and our emotions will be stable. The goal is not to stifle our emotions and shove them in a corner where they won't bother us but to experience the fullness of being in love, pursuing passionately, caring deeply, worshipping in awe and wonder, feeling with others in a way that helps us understand their hurt, or taking off in wild abandonment to discover what it means to truly trust Him.

Emotion also takes over when we're feeling overwhelmed with anxiety or depression. Those consuming emotions have us convinced it's all bad, it will never get better, it's only going to get worse, we're all alone, no one loves us, no one cares, and God isn't there. The simplest task becomes insurmountable. Innocent comments become full-frontal assaults. Everyday decisions appear beyond comprehension.

New game plan. There is no switch to just turn them off. These out of control emotions have to be fully surrendered to Him. "But the fruit of the Spirit is love, joy, peace, patience, kindness, goodness, faithfulness, gentleness, self-control; against such things there is no law. Now those who belong to Christ Jesus have crucified the flesh with its passions and desires." (Galatians 5:22-24 NASB) We can allow Him to change our minds about what we perceive as threats. We can submit our desires and passions to be in line with His will and His Spirit living within us. The result can be an emotional transformation and outpouring of His fruit in our lives: love, joy, peace, patience, kindness, goodness, gentleness, and control over our choices and emotions. Rather than condemn those self-defeating emotions, we can choose to surrender our control and entitlement.

This doesn't mean that if you're experiencing

prolonged clinical depression or severe chronic anxiety that you just need to pray more or be more "faithful". It does mean, as you go through it, you have to give up your right to those things that may not be of God. You have to let go of things that you can't change anyway. You have to relinquish control of things you're not suppose to be controlling. Let your daughter-in-law make those choices without resenting her in your heart. Stop holding on to that comment your pastor made three years ago. Reconnect with that small group you were convinced were out to get you. Let others think and feel and do what they are going to think and feel and do. They don't need your approval or control. And, your existence doesn't rely on their acceptance and approval (in spite of what your insecurity is telling you). Depression and anxiety are enough to deal with without adding all of our other baggage into it.

God, is it possible You have something better planned for me? Is it possible some of what I am holding on to and resenting, You never intended me to carry? Is it possible You have set me free from some of the things I choose to cling to? Is it possible I experience so much emotional turmoil because I don't have the power to subject all things to my will? That's Your job. God, I give up. I give in. Remind me to let go when I try to pick these things back up.

(1) Daniel Goleman, *Emotional Intelligence*, Bantam Books, 1995

Day 22

" *Sanctify them by the truth; Your word is truth.*"

(John 17:17)

Not everything we tell ourselves is true when we are experiencing anxiety or depression. Even when we are not interpreting life through those dark lenses, we tend to tell ourselves many things that are not true.

It doesn't matter if it's true or not, if we think it we are going to feel it. If you think someone stole money from you, you are going to feel angry or resentful. Later, when you find the money in a pants pocket, you feel different - because you think different. We believe what we tell ourselves whether it's true or not.

We believe it because it's our voice we hear inside our heads. If it sounded like a demon-alien telling us something, we would notice that - we wouldn't just accept it as true. We tell ourselves "it's not right, it's not fair, it's not supposed to be this way, he shouldn't have said that, she shouldn't have..." and we believe all of that. We don't think we would "lie" to ourselves.

The other reason we believe what we tell ourselves is because we have been listening to our voice inside our heads our whole lives. That voice has always been there. That's why we don't even catch most of what we're saying to ourselves. The thoughts are there, we hear it and believe it. We just don't always catch that our thoughts or perspective are not rational, accurate, or true. Those thoughts are usually emotional reasoning.

> *"Then you will know the truth, and the truth will set you free."*
> (John 8:32 NIV)

Jesus challenged the Jews who clung to beliefs different than what He taught. He confronted their "truths". *"Why is my language not clear to you? Because you are unable to hear what I say. You belong to your father, the devil, and you want to carry out your father's desires. He was a murderer from the beginning, not holding to the truth, for there is no truth in him. When he lies, he speaks his native language, for he is a liar and the father of lies. Yet because I tell the truth, you do not believe me! Can any of you prove me guilty of sin? If I am telling the truth, why don't you believe me? Whoever belongs to God hears what God says. The reason you do not hear is that you do not belong to God."* (John 8:43-47 NIV)

It's understandable that the religious leaders and the people questioned Jesus' words. They knew Him as the carpenter son of Joseph and Mary from Galilee. Why would He claim to be the Son of God? And many of the Jews did believe. *"When Jesus had finished saying these things, the crowds were amazed at his teaching, because he taught as one who had authority, and not as their teachers of the law."* (Matthew 7:28, 29 NIV) His words were truth and He talked about being set free with that truth. Many of the Pharisees saw it differently. Jesus' words went against their man-made standards of holiness and truth. He was opposed to what they had set up. They didn't want to accept His words as truth because that would mean they would have to let go of what they believed to be true about God, life, love, themselves, purpose, and meaning. They would have to change what it meant to be free. His confrontation wasn't soft; He didn't tiptoe around the truth, "You belong to your father, the devil... there is no truth in him. When he lies, he speaks his native language, for he is a liar and the father of lies."

Teach me Your way, Yahweh,
and I will live by Your truth.
Give me an undivided mind to fear
Your name.
(Psalm 86:11 HCSB)

It can be easy for us to establish our own set of lies. Those are the things we tell ourselves about ourselves, others, or God. We think we know why people do what they do. We think we know the future and we dwell on what will happen. We think we know what others are thinking or what they do when we are not around. We think we can read their minds or know their motives without even talking to them. We can become convinced it's all bad and rarely expect the good. We label things before we know the facts. We have expectations that are often unspoken and based on our own personal beliefs of what is supposed to be. We see life through a negative lens. We stop believing what

God's word says about Him or about us. We start to act as though worrying about something will change our circumstances rather than bringing it to God in faith.

We can challenge those thoughts that are working against us by knowing and applying God's truth, scripture. Are we living and making choices based on our thoughts and feelings or based on what He says in His word? We can believe and live like we can do all things through Christ who strengthens us. We can be confident that God is with us even through the darkest circumstances. We can accept His truth as our standard for truth rather than those thoughts or feelings that repeatedly lead us astray.

Father, You sent Your Son to set me free - Free from dread and fear, free from sin and bondage, free from the world and it's ways, free from the power of sin. Teach me Your ways. Help me to walk in Your truth. Help my mind to be undivided, to be steadfast on You and Your truth. Your truth sets me free from my way of doing things and seeing things.

A Word of Hope for Today: Your Heavenly Father cares for you. He wants you to know truth. He is not playing a game or trying to hide from you. He wants to be found by you and wants you to know and experience real truth.

RATE your thoughts. Challenge those thoughts to see if they are Rational, Accurate, True, and Effective. Is it rational to think others are *always* supposed to see you as *perfect*? Is it rational to think *everyone* will *always* see it your way? Is it accurate to say it *never* works out for you? Is it accurate to think *everyone* is watching you when you walk into the store? Is it true when you think *no one* loves you, *everyone* hates you? It may feel that way sometimes but is it true? Is it effective - will worrying about this change anything in a positive way? Will worrying about this for 10 more minutes or 10 more days fix it? Will dwelling on this and being anxious do anything other than make you more stressed?

Day 23

Why am I so depressed? Why this turmoil within me? Put your hope in God, for I will still praise Him, my Savior and my God. I am deeply depressed; therefore I remember You from the land of Jordan and the peaks of Hermon, from Mount Mizar.

(Psalm 42:5, 6 HCSB)

We pray for loved ones with cancer to be healed. We pray for broken marriages to be restored. We pray for those who are lost or have fallen away to be brought in right relationship with our Heavenly Father. We know that sometimes healing happens; sometimes it doesn't but God is still God.

The same is true for those struggling with clinical depression, bipolar disorder, generalized anxiety, complicated grief, or addiction patterns. We need to continue praying for healing and wholeness. At times, God brings immediate relief or healing. Sometimes, it's more of a process as we see changes or improvements over time. Sometimes, we don't see or experience healing or release but God is still God. He allows the struggle to go on.

For the cancer patient, or their family, this can be disheartening but we can still believe God is faithful and has a plan through all of this. We don't always understand why He does what He does. We believe He has the power to change things but we also know He chooses what is best for us.

For those struggling with depression or extreme

anxiety it can be just as disheartening at times. Mild depression can be an annoyance; we don't feel happy or fulfilled, we feel like we're dragging all of the time, irritability may increase, relationships may become harder to manage but it's not necessarily a major disruption of our lives. Severe depression or intense social anxiety can feel like our lives have come to a screeching halt. In some moments we may not believe we can go on. Severe anxiety can be debilitating as the heart rate speeds up, pressure mounts on the chest, breathing feels impossible, our ability to think almost shuts down, and we are convinced there is no way out. Emotionally, mentally, physically, relationally, and spiritually we shut down.

The cancer patient presses on. The woman feeling abandoned and broken at the end of a marriage finds the strength to keep going. The man drowning in his addictions moves forward, sometimes one small step at a time. The person overwhelmed and feeling defeated by depression or anxiety can find a way to keep on going. Our hope is in God. We will remember Him and continue turning to Him. We will not fear.

God is our refuge and strength, an ever-present help in trouble. Therefore we will not fear, though the earth give way and the mountains fall into the heart of the sea, though its waters roar and foam and the mountains quake with their surging.

(Psalm 46:1-3)

The Lord sustains them on their sickbed and restores them from their bed of illness. I said, "Have mercy on me, Lord; heal me, for I have sinned against you."

(Psalm 41:3, 4)

I waited patiently for the Lord; he turned to me and heard my cry. He lifted me out of the slimy pit, out of the mud and mire; he set my feet on a rock and gave me a firm place to stand. He put a new song in my mouth, a hymn of praise to our God. Many will see and fear the Lord and put their trust in him. (Psalm 40:1-3 NIV)

If we allow Him, He will put a new song in our hearts. He lifts us up out of the deep dark pit. He brings healing and comfort. He restores us. He strengthens us. Rescue may not come in the form we are looking for. Sometimes it is just one step, one day, one hour at a time. He leads us through the desert. We have to stay close to Him. The new song comes because of Him not just because the pain stops. We're happy when the pain stops but sometimes it feels like the mountains keep falling around us.

Can I learn to trust You with the bad and not just the good?

This is where we have to believe over and over again that God is our Rock, He is our strength, He is our hope, He is our strong tower, He is our mighty warrior, He is our defender and protector and redeemer and healer. He is our salvation. He is our good Shepherd. He is our righteousness and our refuge and our shelter. He is our light. He is our Heavenly Father. Life does not make sense centered around us. It's never enough, there always has to be more, there's always something wrong with someone or something. Life only makes sense centered around Him and even then *our* emotions can work against us to pull us back into orbit around us. Emotional gravity.

God, *You are the center. It all revolves around You. Praise comes because we recognize it is about You, not us.*

He put a new song in my mouth,
a song of praise to our God;
Many will see and fear
and will trust in the Lord
(Psalms 40:3 NASB)

It doesn't make sense. Cancer eating the body, addictions craving the unobtainable, depression blocking the sun, fear feeding more fear, anxiety stomping out reality, violence ripping apart families, anger crushing dreams, sin covering hope and smothering life. Defeat drives the bus and we have to choose to get off. If not, we'll end up wherever it takes us.

This is when He gives us a new song. A song that may only come because we are broken and weak and alone. A song that is the cry of our hearts and our pain. A song that grabs on to our one true hope. A song that is our response to His voice. This may be how we learn to praise in the middle of the muck and the mire as our praise is focused on Him.

Father, give me a new song to sing to You. Help me to be content and fulfilled in You. Help me to believe invincibly, without any ounce of doubt, that You are more than able to do all that I ask or imagine and yet also believe, without a doubt, that You will do what is right and I am safe in You. Give me a new song. A song of hope and strength.

A Word of Hope for Today: Be confident that you are His child; He loves you passionately and fully with an everlasting love. Spend time in His presence. Let His peace calm your spirit. Let His hope warm you and comfort you. Let His strength carry you. Sing to the Lord a new song. Open your heart and see what comes out.

Day 24

Consider it a great joy, my brothers, whenever you experience various trials, knowing that the testing of your faith produces endurance. But endurance must do its complete work, so that you may be mature and complete, lacking nothing.

Now if any of you lacks wisdom, he should ask God, who gives to all generously and without criticizing, and it will be given to him. But let him ask in faith without doubting. For the doubter is like the surging sea, driven and tossed by the wind. That person should not expect to receive anything from the Lord. An indecisive man is unstable in all his ways. (James 1:2-8 HCSB)

Where do we turn when we are overcome with dread or anxiety? Our God is our hope. James 1:2-5 can be a comforting focus. James gives us the calm assurance that everything is going to be ok. He doesn't say that it will be easy or all of our problems will disappear but there is a confidence that we can consider our troubling circumstances as great joy.

It would be very unsettling if James had written to fellow believers and told them to be afraid. Be very afraid. Instead he encouraged them (and us) to consider various trials and hardships as joy, pure joy. He didn't even know what it was they (and us) were facing. It didn't matter. His confidence wasn't in our ability or how small the problem would be. His confidence was in how big God is. The size or length or strength or duration of the problem did not determine how or if we might get through it.

When our response is to accept these difficulties with joy rather than fear, dread, or stress, we move forward with more confidence and trust. We can face that next anxiety attack with quiet peace because we know it will stretch and strengthen our faith. We can press on through those dark days of depression when we're struggling to get out of bed because we're convinced that God is using even this in a relevant, real, and intentional step to help me grow closer to Him. We can face the unexpected crises today with confidence, watching to see Him at work in our lives.

That we can consider difficult times as joyful is our assurance that there is a master plan behind what happens and He is able to use all of it for His holy purposes. He is personally intervening in our lives and wants us to find Him. We can be confident that everything and anything happening in our lives can be redeemed, restored, and used by Him.

You will seek me and find me

when you seek me

with all your heart.

(Jeremiah 29:13)

Faith in Him is to be our response when crisis happens. Faith in His ability and faith in His character. *"... because you know that the testing of your faith produces perseverance. Let perseverance finish its work so that you may be mature and complete, not lacking anything."* (James 1:3, 4 NIV)

"This is what the Lord says: 'When seventy years are completed for Babylon, I will come to you and fulfill my good promise to bring you back to this place. For I know the plans I have for you,' declares the Lord, 'plans to prosper you and not to harm you, plans to give you hope and a future. Then you will call on me and come and pray to me, and I will listen to you. You will seek me and find me when you seek me with all your heart. I will be found by you,' declares the Lord, 'and will bring you back from captivity. I will gather you from all the nations and places where I have banished you,' declares the Lord, 'and will bring you back to the place from which I carried you into exile.'" (Jer. 29:10-14 NIV)

This is not the genie-in-a-bottle verse that some make it out to be. It's not a feel-good guarantee that nothing bad will ever happen. The Israelites had been in captivity for almost seventy years and as they returned to the Lord and put their faith in His promises, He brought them out of captivity and restored the people and Jerusalem.

We have a difficult time considering seventy years in bondage and slavery as a great joy. It's great to be set free, it doesn't feel great while we're going through the muck and the mire. God did not abandon His people during the captivity but they felt abandoned. He did not cause the suffering but they felt it just the same.

You may be looking for relief from depression or anxiety, keep seeking Him through it. Keep taking the steps you need to take. Be faithful with where He has you and what He's given you. Keep trusting His word, keep praying diligently, and keep your eyes on Him. Keep believing He is with you regardless of what you're going through. Keep your hope and faith in Him not just in what He can do for you. His promise is not to just make it all go away but to be with you through it all. His word to us is to consider it a gift, receive it with joy, rather than solely trying to get out if it. This is being single-minded rather than double-minded.

"Consider it a sheer gift, friends, when tests and challenges come at you from all sides. You know that under pressure, your faith-life is forced into the open and shows its true colors. So don't try to get out of anything prematurely. Let it do its work so you become mature and well-developed, not deficient in any way."
(James 1:2-4 The Message)

But how does this depression help me grow if every day I feel defeated, deflated, discouraged, and depressed? How is it helping me if overwhelming anxiety or fear sets in every time I think of going to the store or there is a project due? Suffering is not the goal but our reaction to it is what grows us and gives it purpose. Each experience is an opportunity to exercise our faith.

"Not only so, but we also glory in our sufferings, because we know that suffering produces perseverance; perseverance, character; and character, hope. And hope does not put us to shame, because God's love has been poured out into our hearts through the Holy Spirit, who has been given to us." (Romans 5:3-5 NIV)

Suffering does not mean that He has abandoned us or fallen down in the job. When the Lord God chooses to take these afflictions from us, He is glorified. He is compassionate and loving and does what is best for His children. When He chooses to leave the afflictions and walk with us through these, He is glorified. He is still choosing to do what is best for us. He is glorified as we endure and find our hope and strength in Him.

" For I know the plans I have for

you," declares the Lord,

"plans to prosper you

and not to harm you,

plans to give you hope and a future.
(Jeremiah 29:11 NIV)

Even though these times are difficult they will not destroy us. That's what these three passages have in common. It is difficult but not destructive. He allows it to build us up and transform us. If we don't see our circumstances from this perspective, we have to change our perspective to line up with His truth. We have to change rather than focusing so hard on changing the circumstances or trying to get God to change.

God, sometimes I have a difficult time seeing the good in what I am going through. Sometimes it feels unfair or unjust. Help me to re-align what is right and just according to Your word. Help me to trust that You are in control, that You have my ultimate good in mind. Help me to consider it all joy and to find my rest in You.

A Word of Hope for Today: He says, "Be still, and know that I am God; I will be exalted among the nations, I will be exalted in the earth." The Lord Almighty is with us; the God of Jacob is our fortress. (Psalm 46:10,11) Be still and quiet and wait on Him. The NASB words it this way, "Cease striving". The HCSB translates it "stop your fighting – and know that I am God."

Day 25

For even when we came into Macedonia our flesh had no rest, but we were afflicted on every side: conflicts without, fears within. But God, who comforts the depressed, comforted us by the coming of Titus; and not only by his coming, but also by the comfort with which he was comforted in you, as he reported to us your longing, your mourning, your zeal for me; so that I rejoiced even more. For though I caused you sorrow by my letter, I do not regret it; though I did regret it- for I see that that letter caused you sorrow, though only for a while- I now rejoice, not that you were made sorrowful, but that you were made sorrowful to the point of repentance; for you were made sorrowful according to the will of God, so that you might not suffer loss in anything through us. For the sorrow that is according to the will of God produces a repentance without regret, leading to salvation, but the sorrow of the world produces death. (2 Corinthians 7:5-10 NASB)

There is an appointed time for everything. And there is a time for every event under

heaven – a time to weep and a time to laugh;
A time to mourn and a time to dance.

(Ecclesiastes 3:1, 4 NASB)

It is better to go to a house of mourning than to go to a house of feasting, for death is the destiny of everyone; the living should take this to heart. Frustration is better than laughter, because a sad face is good for the heart.

(Ecclesiastes 7:2, 3 NIV)

The NIV says, "a sad face is good for the heart." It's not good for the heart when we are sad or depressed or anxious on the inside but on the outside we put on the fake smile. It can be easy for good faithful Christians to think that's what we're supposed to do. Aren't we supposed to be joyful through difficult times?

There's a difference between finding joy in trials and being emotionally dishonest with ourselves, God, or others. If we're fake and act like we have it all together when we really don't, we're side-stepping the problems and avoiding emotional honesty. What others think of us becomes the primer for us to feel good about ourselves rather than genuinely working through the difficulty. Immediate emotional gratification leads us away from dealing with the real issues at hand.

Paul addressed this with the believers in Corinth. They were not happy with Paul and his snappy little letters. Paul was ok with them being upset with him because it led to real change, change at a deep heart level.   Rather than writing fluffy little feel-good messages, he addressed the real heart issues and they responded. They weren't bad people but they were not doing as they should on some areas. Paul was willing to call them on this.   Healthy boundaries. They didn't like it but they responded well. Eventually. A sad face is good for the heart.

Their sadness and honesty brought about repentance. Transformation. "For the sorrow that is according to the will of God produces a repentance without regret." (v. 10) God allows our struggle because it brings about transformation. Another way of saying this is that we can be honest with Him about our sadness, our depressed feelings, our fear, regret, stress, and our pain. He knows it's there. He understands and can see the end result behind it. We can be transparent and vulnerable with Him, knowing that He is our strength. In our weakness, He is strong. When we act like we have it all together and we have no problems, we are not acting out of faith but self-sufficiency.

... for death is the destiny of everyone;

the living should take this to heart.

(Ecclesiastes 7:2b NIV)

A "sad face" doesn't mean that we walk around acting like a victim or martyr all the time. It's not an excuse to wallow in our self-pity. It also doesn't mean that we give up and let this become our defeated identity. Life happens. There are real concerns that affect our lives. Our response to those determines if we are transformed by these or defeated by these.

Solomon reminds us that "death is the destiny of everyone." We should live with the awareness that life has pain. There are some things we cannot control. Our hope is in the belief that there is a bigger picture. Jesus takes us from death to life. Jesus gives us new life in Him. Jesus empowers us to live and face these struggles with Him inside of us.

There is sadness and pain and worry; real life circumstances that cause sad faces, broken hearts, and deep wounds. It's a reality we are not immune from. If we can be honest about this with ourselves and with God, He can bring healing. Part of the healing is admitting the need. If we cover it up or excuse it away, we go on nursing our wounds but never move beyond them. Worldly sorrow leads to death and loss. It is about feeling bad but no transformation is involved.

Therefore humble yourselves under the mighty hand of God, that He may exalt you at the proper time, casting all your anxiety on Him, because He cares for you.
(1 Peter 5:6, 7 NASB)

God does not instruct us to smile and act like nothing is wrong. Jesus was very transparent and vulnerable with His struggles. We know He wept for His friend Lazarus. We know He wanted the Father to take the cross from Him. We know He was moved with compassion when He saw the crowds of people in need.

He doesn't instruct us to put on the façade of good holy church people with no sense of power, meaning, or purpose. He instructs us to bring our concerns to Him, to live lives that are set apart for Him, to be His people, and to humble ourselves before Him. "Therefore humble yourselves under the mighty hand of God, that He may exalt you at the proper time, casting all your anxiety on Him, because He cares for you." (1 Peter 5:6, 7 NASB) Is anyone among you suffering? He should pray. Is anyone cheerful? He should sing praises. (James 5:13 HCSB)

Thank You, Lord, that you know my hurt, You understand my pain. You long for me to come to You, just as I am. You know my sad face, whether others see it or not. It does not diminish You or Your glory if I struggle. I can be humble and honest and open with You. Transform this sad face into a full, content heart, satisfied with You. Life is fast and fleeting, the world keeps spinning, death and pain are a reality but there is fullness of life in You.

A Word of Hope for Today: Jesus wept. Our Heavenly Father grieves, He understands. Bring your fears or worries or pain to Him. Write out what you are thinking and feeling. Be honest with yourself and God. A sad face is good for the heart when it leads to vulnerability and transparency to be healed.

Day 26

There is an appointed time for everything. And there is a time for every event under heaven – a time to weep and a time to laugh; A time to mourn and a time to dance.

(Ecclesiastes 3:1, 4 NASB)

A cheerful heart is good medicine, but a crushed spirit dries up the bones.

(Proverbs 17:22)

When the LORD brought back the captive ones of Zion, We were like those who dream. Then our mouth was filled with laughter and our tongue with joyful shouting; then they said among the nations, "The LORD has done great things for them." The LORD has done great things for us; we are glad.

(Psalm 126:1-3 NASB)

What makes God laugh? When He laughs, does He roll around on the floor with a full, whole-hearted chortle and His belly bouncing in rhythm to His uncontrollable cackles? Does it vibrate through every aspect of His being? You would think if it's something so funny even God finds it humorous, it's got to be funny. He does express His amusement but His perception of what is amusing may be different than ours.

"The wicked plot against the righteous and gnash

their teeth at them; but the Lord laughs at the wicked, for he knows their day is coming." (Psalm 37:12, 13 NIV)

"The kings of the earth rise up and the rulers band together against the Lord and against his anointed, saying, 'Let us break their chains and throw off their shackles.' The One enthroned in heaven laughs; the Lord scoffs at them." (Psalm 2:2-4 NIV)

He laughs at the wicked. He sees the scheming plans of man and finds it funny that man thinks he can stand on his own without God. We think it's funny when the cat falls into the toilet or the teenager runs into the closed glass doors. *America's Funniest Video* show was mostly physical mishaps caught on video. Sometimes painful, sometimes awkward or embarrassing. It was funny because it didn't happen to us. Bill Cosby can take the everyday events of life and find the humor in them. In the 90's, we watched a comedy show about nothing. Jim Gaffigan draws our attention to bacon and *Hot Pockets, "the only thing better than bacon is bacon wrapped in bacon."* Of course, we have to hear the nuances of their delivery to make it funny but there are humorous moments in life. We like to laugh... most of the time. God laughs at the absurdity that we think we can live life meaningfully without Him. That can be painful as well.

A cheerful heart is good medicine,
but a crushed spirit dries up the bones.
(Proverbs 17:22)

Laughter is great medicine. Humor and laughter

make life more enjoyable and make us more enjoyable. Research has shown that laughter also has other healthy and helpful effects. Researcher Sven Svebak of the medical school at Norwegian University of Science and Technology studied the effects of laughter on 54,000 Norwegians for seven years. Patients who laughed more were 35% more likely to live longer.

According to the Mayo Institute, laughter triggers healthy physical reactions such as strengthening the immune system, boosting energy levels, decreasing the effects of stress, and diminishing pain. Laughter releases endorphins in the body that helps reduce pain. Laughter creates more social connectivity. We're drawn to people who laugh more. Sometimes we use it to deflate tense situations. Laughing helps us not take ourselves too seriously. *If we can't laugh at ourselves, others will.* In 2011, Psychology Today reported that "the average four-year-old laughs 300 times a day, a 40-year-old, only four." That says a lot about taking ourselves too seriously. Laughter is also a natural way to reduce stress and anxiety. *Laughter helps us to see a different perspective on situations.* Research out of the University of Denver found that married couples that had fun and laughed together were happier and more content in life.

Can we laugh when we realize our expectations may not be in line with His? Can we be serious about what He is serious about so that we can laugh at what does not matter? Life can be serious. There are many things that will consume our time, thoughts, and energy. Some situations or conditions aren't fun, funny, or laughable. We need to know how to weep, to grieve, to empathize with others.

But, there are also some situations where we need to see the humor. According to Wikipedia, in the animal world, only a few animals have been found to laugh: dogs, rats, and a few types of primates. I'm not sure what rats have to laugh about but maybe they can rejoice in all situations. I haven't heard too many dogs tell any really good jokes lately and I'm not sure if hyenas laugh but they mimic the sound. Humans laugh. We find humor in such a wide variety of areas and it's very subjective.

Blessed are you who weep now,
for you will laugh.
(Luke 6:21b)

And God laughs. Made in His image, we acquire that trait. Just not always at the appropriate things. Research on laughter indicates that it is healthy and beneficial for us to laugh. Sometimes, we need to be intentional to find humor and allow ourselves to laugh even when everything around us is shutting down. Besides the healthy physical effects, it affects our emotions. It's a natural way to change the body's chemistry.

You turned my wailing into dancing;
you removed my sackcloth
and clothed me with joy.
(Psalm 30:11)

The goal is not to laugh everything off and take nothing serious. Some issues we need to face head-on rather than avoiding them and hoping they will disappear. We may be over-focused on other concerns and taking ourselves too seriously. His goal may not be to take away all of the circumstances. His goal is not for us to be happy all of the time. His desire for us is bigger than that. He allows the struggles but also provides the healing and overcoming. And our response is to rejoice, to count it as joyful, to let Him turn our "wailing into dancing" and our sorrow into joy. If He is the Center, we should be able to laugh and dance and be joyful as we see Him moving in our lives.

It is difficult to laugh when bills are pressing, there is no relief in sight, and we've just been struck another blow. The dark depths of depression affect our perspective – nothing seems funny. We don't see the humor. The black cloud overshadows everything and we don't have the energy to laugh. It takes too much effort. We're drained. Depression is self-feeding. The more it can make us think there is no hope, no light, or no glimmer, the deeper the depression gets. The cycle perpetuates. This is the time to allow ourselves to laugh. Disrupt the pattern. Have fun – even though we may have to push through every action, take the step.

Father, Help me to laugh even when there seems to be nothing to laugh at. Bring healing to this heart that feels overwhelmed and struggles to find the good in anything. Help me to rejoice in You.

A Word of Hope for Today: Your Heavenly Father knows the pain or worry or sadness that you carry. He doesn't laugh or mock your pain but He feels it with you. He wants you to experience real freedom in Him and to find joy.

Be intentional to find healthy things to laugh at. Take the time to go see a funny movie, buy a book of jokes or funny stories, spend an evening with fun friends, or look through your old high school pictures. Laughter is free. And healthy.

Day 27

Bless the LORD, O my soul, And all that is within me, bless His holy name. Bless the LORD, O my soul, And forget none of His benefits; Who pardons all your iniquities, Who heals all your diseases; Who redeems your life from the pit, Who crowns you with lovingkindness and compassion; Who satisfies your years with good things, So that your youth is renewed like the eagle. The LORD performs righteous deeds And judgments for all who are oppressed.

(Psalm 103:1-6 NASB)

"When peace like a river attendeth my way. When sorrows like sea billows roll. Whatever my lot thou hast taught me to say it is well, it is well with my soul."

You may be familiar with the story behind this classic hymn. Following the death of his four daughters, Horatio Spafford wrote the hymn while at sea as he sailed past the spot were his daughters died in a ship wreck. His wife survived the wreck but their four daughters did not. Three years prior to this, the Spaffords lost a four-year-old son to scarlet fever. They then suffered financial loss. Spafford never seemed to lose faith in his God. The hymn is a declaration of his choice to rest securely in his Father's arms regardless of the tragedy he faced.

"Though Satan should buffet, though trials should come, Let this blest assurance control, That Christ hath regarded my helpless estate, And hath shed His own blood for my soul."

"Though Satan should buffet, though trials should come..." It can be difficult to say and to mean, "whatever my lot, Thou hast taught me to say, it is well with my soul." We're not so fond of "whatever my lot..." or "though trials should come". That's too open-ended and beyond our control. That leaves too much to His imagination and not enough to our abilities. Self-sufficiency has a way of emasculating our faith. Even good, well intentioned, prosperous Christians can appear loving, resourceful, and obedient but be void of real faith. "It is well with my soul" is a confession of our dependency on Him. No matter what we are going through or what we fear we will face, our hope and faith are in Him. Our faith and trust are in His ability and His character.

Now to him who is able to do immeasurably more than all we ask or imagine, according to his power that is at work within us.
(Ephesians 3:20 NIV)

We have to believe that He is able to do what He has said He would do. *"Now to him who is able to do immeasurably more than all we ask or imagine, according to his power that is at work within us"* (Ephesians 3:20 NIV). *"Who, by the power that enables him to bring everything under his control, will transform our lowly bodies so that they will be like his glorious body."* (Philippians 3:21 NIV). *"And we know that in all things God works for the good of those who love him, who have been called according to his purpose."* (Romans 8:28 NIV). Our faith and trust are in His ability not ours. We choose to believe He has the power to not only change our circumstances but to transform our lives.

Not only do we trust He is able to handle whatever our lot may be, we have to trust in His character. We have to believe He is good and only wants what is ultimately good for us. We have to believe He is love and acts in genuine love towards us. We accept and believe He is holy and He cannot act in ways that go against His holy character. We trust Him to do that which builds us up and does not tear us down. What we face may be difficult but not destructive. This is putting our faith in who He is, His character. We trust He cannot lie. *"So that by two unchangeable things in which it is impossible for God to lie, we who have taken refuge would have strong encouragement to take hold of the hope set before us."* (Hebrews 6:18 NASB)

Depression has a way of shaking us and leading us to believe the worst. It's easy to believe we're alone, defeated, rejected, unloved, doomed, and stuck. Anxious thoughts can feel like an attack as we tell ourselves it will not work out, we will fail, others will see all of our faults, or we have to be perfect. We rerun every "what if..." worst-case scenario. The consuming thoughts and exasperating emotions can collude, collide, and culminate in an explosion of self-reliance, self-defeat, and penniless faith.

Now faith is the assurance
of things hoped for,
the conviction of things not seen.
(Hebrews 11:1 NASB)

Emotions and thoughts can overpower even the strongest faith. But faith is also how we counter those attacks. Faith is believing in what we don't see or feel. "Now faith is the assurance of things hoped for, the conviction of things not seen." (Hebrews 11:1 NASB) We choose not to believe those misguided thoughts or to be jerked around by the onslaught of runaway emotions. We choose to walk by faith not by sight (2 Cor. 5:7). Faith is not based on a feeling. God is not with us simply because we feel like He is with us. He is with us in spite of our feelings. Our faith is not based on how we feel or what we think, it is based on His truth not ours.

When you're really honest with yourself, what do you tell yourself about God? About His faithfulness? About His love for you? About your worthiness? Are those feelings and thoughts grounded in His truth or your emotions and experience? How loved do you feel? How does your degree of feeling loved taint your perceptions?

Father, thank You for Your faithfulness, Your goodness, and Your compassion. Help me to fully trust You today with "whatever my lot" may be. When anxious thoughts invade, help me to trust in You and grab on to Your truth, knowing that I am secure in You. When hopeless thoughts or overwhelming emotions seem to want to take control of my life and my soul, help me to say confidently, "it is well with my soul."

A Word of Hope for Today: You are precious to God. He loves you with an everlasting love. He is able to handle whatever you face today. Your thoughts or emotions may tell you different. You may think or feel that your circumstances or experiences are proof that He does not love you or will not help you. Catch those thoughts as they pop up. Challenge those thoughts with God's word. It's ok to admit that some of your thoughts don't line up with His word. Not admitting it perpetuates the pattern. Faith is the step you take to believe His word even when it doesn't feel true – it's based on what we can't see or feel.

The earth is the Lord's, and everything in it, the world, and all who live in it; for he founded it on the seas and established it on the waters. Who may ascend the mountain of the Lord? Who may stand in his holy place? The one who has clean hands and a pure heart, who does not trust in an idol or swear by a false god.

(Psalm 24:1-4 NIV)

" and Nebuchadnezzar said to them, "Is it true, Shadrach, Meshach and Abednego, that you do not serve my gods or worship the image of gold I have set up? Now when you hear the sound of the horn, flute, zither, lyre, harp, pipe and all kinds of music, if you are ready to fall down and worship the image I made, very good. But if you do not worship it, you will be thrown immediately into a blazing furnace. Then what god will be able to rescue you from my hand?" Shadrach, Meshach and Abednego replied to him, "King Nebuchadnezzar, we do not need to defend ourselves before you in this matter. If we are thrown into the blazing furnace, the God we serve is able to deliver us from it, and he will deliver us from Your Majesty's hand. But even if he does not, we want you to know, Your Majesty, that we will not serve your gods or worship the image of gold you have set up." (Daniel 3:14-18 *NIV*)

There can be a fine line between desperation and faith. We all experience those moments when we desperately want God to act and we know He can do it but He may choose not to. Everything in us is frantic for Him to respond but... Back and forth between what our heart wants and accepting that His heart may want something different. When we settle in that place where we are content with His will over ours we know that He will get us through whatever He allows.

Some things are easier to accept than others. That promotion at work would have meant more opportunities, more money, and we think we've earned it. Then it goes to someone else. It can be a bitter pill to swallow but we can be thankful we have a job and income. We can move on. It's a different story for that person who hasn't worked for the past four years, their employer downsized, the mortgage is in foreclosure, the other bills are piling up, they are doing any available side job to literally put food on the table, and now the car needs repairs but they can't even afford to buy gas. On top of that, the middle child is not getting the therapy they desperately need. A new job opportunity means something different to that person.

There's a desperation that can set in. We experience it sometimes when there has been an unexpected tragedy, a loved one is dying, a violent relationship gets worse rather than better, a critical illness hits, or a chronic condition never seems to improve or resolve. We know of loved ones hurting or suffering through dreadful circumstances. We hear of impending doom that will dramatically impact and interrupt our lives or the lives of those we love. Often our immediate response is to avoid pain or disruption or discomfort.

"Thrown into the blazing furnace" sounds like a game changer. It's a little more than a broken finger nail. Shadrach, Meshach and Abednego were facing a crisis situation. They didn't cause it but it was still happening. It was not the result of poor choices, unhealthy relationships, or even the consequences of sin. They were doing what they thought was right and what honored their God.

> *"But even if He does not,*
> *let it be known to you,*
> *O king, that we are not going to*
> *serve your gods*
> *or worship the golden image*
> *that you have set up."*
> (Daniel 3:18 NASB)

Sometimes we have to accept "it is what it is". We pray diligently, the situation doesn't change, and we walk by faith through it. We learn to endure. Persevere. *"Not only so, but we also glory in our sufferings, because we know that suffering produces perseverance; perseverance, character; and character, hope. And hope does not put us to shame, because God's love has been poured out into our hearts through the Holy Spirit, who has been given to us."* (Romans 5:3-5 NIV)

You would think that hope would come first. That we would hope things will get better, we stick with it, and character is built through the experience. Paul tells us "suffering produces perseverance; perseverance, character; and character, hope." For believers, hope is more than luck or wishful thinking. Our hope is in a specific person. We're not stuck with "maybe He will or maybe He won't" and then He flips a coin to decide what to do. He always acts in accordance with His divine will. Our hope and trust are in Him to be who He says He is.

We can be hopeful. Full of hope. Even through the darkest situations. Our hope is in Him.

God does not tell us to give up, blindly give in, or just accept whatever comes our way. He wants us to persevere, to press on, to endure, to be full of faith, full of hope, full of Him. *"But he must ask in faith without any doubting, for the one who doubts is like the surf of the sea, driven and tossed by the wind. For that man ought not to expect that he will receive anything from the Lord, being a double-minded man, unstable in all his ways."* (James 1:6-8 NASB).

That's the delicate balance - to believe without doubting that He will come through on this thing that we so desperately need and yet content in Him if He chooses not to. Shadrach, Meshach and Abednego knew He was able to deliver them and they believed He would. Our Heavenly Father wants us to depend on Him, to put our trust in Him, to turn to Him with our cries and longing. He wants to move in our lives and show Himself strong. It's not like we have to convince Him or trick Him into helping us. He wants us to find our hope and strength and peace in Him. Why would He not answer our prayers - when we are in line with His will? But He also wants us to pursue after Him rather than just what we can get from Him.

"I am the vine;
you are the branches.
If you remain in me and I in you,
you will bear much fruit;
apart from me you can do nothing."
(John 15:5 NIV)

"I am the vine, you are the branches; he who abides in Me and I in him, he bears much fruit, for apart from Me you can do nothing. If anyone does not abide in Me, he is thrown away as a branch and dries up; and they gather them, and cast them into the fire and they are burned. If you abide in Me, and My words abide in you, ask whatever you wish, and it will be done for you. My Father is glorified by this, that you bear much fruit, and so prove to be My disciples. Just as the Father has loved Me, I have also loved you; abide in My love." (John 15:5-9 NASB)

Sometimes it's the huge tragedy that hits us out of nowhere. It may be the loss of a limb, the loss of a loved one, or the loss of a relationship. Sometimes, it's the persistent, chronic situation or condition that wears us down. Depression can be like that. Others may not understand how it can feel so bad or why don't we just... And the answer is we can't. It feels like a thick, dark fog suffocating us and all of our energy is exhausted on just surviving. Our thoughts are either non-stop and overwhelming or our thoughts have come to a screeching halt. We don't want to talk or make decisions or think about anything. Sleeping becomes a way to avoid all of that. We've prayed and believed it would get better. We've stepped out in faith. We may have even fasted and had others pray over us. When the dark cloud doesn't go away, it's easy to give up hope and stop believing it can or will change.

Our "hope" is not that we'll feel better; our hope is in Him. We want to feel better and should keep believing we will feel better. In our suffering, our encouragement from Paul is to "glory in our sufferings, because we know that suffering produces perseverance; perseverance, character; and character, hope. And hope does not put us to shame, because God's love has been poured out into our hearts through the Holy Spirit, who has been given to us."

God is at work in us through all that we are going through. He has given us His Spirit, which is alive and active in us through the suffering. "Our hope does not put us to shame." We don't lose by being faithful. Persevering through each day's struggling is the next right thing to do, regardless of how it turns out. Our character is shaped by this. In faith terms, He is refining and strengthening us, producing hope.

It would be easy to think that Shadrach, Meshach and Abednego were faithful because they knew God was going to rescue them but they didn't know that. The fiery furnace wasn't the only struggle they faced. The Israelites had been in captivity for years. We can assume they were praying for deliverance from bondage and it didn't happen immediately. Their hope was not diminished because they were still in captivity. They persevered and remained faithful. Even in captivity, they were confident in their God. Their character was strengthened and their hope was fortified before they reached the furnace. They knew their God was able, they whole-heartedly proclaimed He would rescue them, but they also knew He could choose not to. Whatever direction, He would be with them.

You may have been dealing with depression and anxiety for years. It may feel like it will never change and you may be wondering if God hears your prayers. Stay Faithful. Be confident in Him.

The Lord was glorified as Daniel interpreted the king's dreams. God was glorified as the captives remained faithful to their diet in chapter one. He was glorified as Daniel was delivered from the mouths of lions. He was glorified as Shadrach, Meshach and Abednego were protected from the scorching flames. Some prayers were answered, some were not but God was faithful to them through it all.

God of all creation, continue to be my strength. I put my trust in You. What I am experiencing feels overwhelming but I believe You are more than able to handle it and to get me through this. Whether You choose to heal or deliver me, I will worship only You.

A Word of Hope for Today: you may feel like you're facing the fiery furnace and it's just been cranked up another seven notches. You may be facing a tragic situation that appears hopeless and painful. You may be suffering through a chronic condition that seems it will never let up. Be encouraged, your God has not forgotten you or forsaken you. Be hope-full, believe whole-heartedly He is able to deliver you through this. Be faith-full, regardless of the direction the circumstances take you, continue to do the next right thing. Remain in Him as He remains in you. Captivity may not be over in a day but He will strengthen you and encourage you and lead you step by step. Keep your eyes focused on Him, not just what He can do for you. We are called to believe whole-heartedly, that He will intervene and to believe whole-heartedly that if He does not, He is still more than enough for us.

Day 29

"This is what the Lord says: "Stand at the crossroads and look; ask for the ancient paths, ask where the good way is, and walk in it, and you will find rest for your souls. But you said, 'We will not walk in it.' I appointed watchmen over you and said, 'Listen to the sound of the trumpet!' But you said, 'We will not listen.' Therefore hear, you nations; you who are witnesses, observe what will happen to them. Hear, you earth: I am bringing disaster on this people, the fruit of their schemes, because they have not listened to my words and have rejected my law. What do I care about incense from Sheba or sweet calamus from a distant land? Your burnt offerings are not acceptable; your sacrifices do not please me." Therefore this is what the Lord says: "I will put obstacles before this people. Parents and children alike will stumble over them; neighbors and friends will perish."

Jeremiah 6:16-21

We have to be prepared for the unexpected. We have to be prepared for change. Most of us want to get back to normal. Our normal. Can we believe God is doing a work in us and what we are now going through is part of the process? If His goal is transformation, why would He take us back to where we were before?

We can embrace change. It's why we got saved. The way we were before was not ok and we needed to be rescued. From ourselves. He didn't save us just to keep us the same. We needed to be renewed, redeemed, revived, transformed, and reclaimed. He took us from death to life, from darkness to light, from bondage to freedom. And then we fight hard to stay the same. We like the freedom, the light, and the life but not necessarily the changes that come with it.

He wants to do a fresh work in our hearts; to help us let go of those old patterns that make us think everything was just fine the way it was before. God is using this depression or anxiety or stressful situation to help us experience more abundant life in Him. Is the goal to work through this depression just to return to our old lives? Or, is the goal to be changed through these circumstances? Sometimes I just want to feel better. Thank God, He has a bigger plan in mind.

In their hearts humans

plan their course,

but the Lord

establishes their steps.

(Proverbs 16:9 NIV)

We need to examine our hearts and our lives. Is there sin in our lives? Are there selfish patterns we will not give up? Is there depression, un-forgiveness, isolation, anxiety, fear, or resentment because of sin that has subtly crept in and become the new normal? Are we holding on to something that keeps us locked in a pattern of depression or fear or self-reliance? Are we taking responsibility for people who are not our responsibility? Are we afraid of what they might say or do? Are we controlling others because of our fears or insecurities? Are we depressed and resentful because we refuse to let go of wrongs done to us? Have we been unwilling to be loving, forgiving, or compassionate? Do we stay depressed because it's easier than taking responsibility for our selves or it maintains our status as the victim? Is there something God has set us free from but we keep running back to it? Are we resistant to His will? Am I living in my own strength and "wisdom" or His? These are some of the things He may be refining out of us.

"The Lord makes firm the steps of the one who delights in him; though he may stumble, he will not fall, for the Lord upholds him with his hand. I was young and now I am old, yet I have never seen the righteous forsaken or their children begging bread." (Psalm 37:23-25 NIV)

Depression or anxiety are not a punishment for a lack of faith. But they may be a result of not living a life of faith: when we trust in our own abilities, when we become overly dependent on others for approval, acceptance, happiness, or our existence, or when we have given up and choose to believe He is not who He says He is. We stop believing He is working in our favor.

The Lord God spoke to Jeremiah and pointed out how the people resisted His voice. They fell and struggled when they went their own ways. We know that in Christ there is freedom, there is no condemnation, we are made right with God but do we continue to live like we are not in Christ? If we continue to see ourselves as in bondage, we will continue to live in bondage and if we continue to live in bondage, we will continue to see ourselves in bondage. It's an exhausting cycle.

Stand at the crossroads and look;

ask for the ancient paths,

ask where the good way is,

and walk in it,

and you will find

rest for your souls.

(Jeremiah 6:16)

Examine your heart. Stand at the crossroads and look. Ask where the good way is and walk in it. *Ask yourself what is the next right thing to do.* For some it may be to just go walking every day. Do something physical. Play ball. Walk by the lake. Play tennis again. For some it may be to get out of bed. Avoid going back to bed. Be honest with yourself that you sleep to avoid life. Get up and move. Commit to take a shower and get dressed every day. For some it may be to cut off those unhealthy relationships. Avoid negative conversations. Put a stop to the toxic, co-dependent relationship. Seek out others who will invest in you. Encourage others. Re-connect with those you've been avoiding. Apologize. For some it may be to pray for forgiveness. Spend time in the Word. Spend time in prayer. Spend time in fellowship. Attend a worship service. Open up and truly praise. Give often and freely. Ask for wisdom and direction. Admit you can't do it on your own. Hide His word in your heart. Meditate on it day and night. Fast and seek His face. Pray for others. Ask others to pray for you. Accept His truth as truth. Rest in His provision. Delight yourself in Him. For some it may be to seek out a pastor or therapist. Find help. Admit there's a problem. Be vulnerable. Learn your strengths. Take off the mask. Challenge the negative, distorted thoughts. Write out a list. Join an accountability group. Take a step. Open up about the secrets. Be aware of how defensive or anxious you react. Name your emotions. List your fears. Be honest about what's not working in your life.

A man's steps are determined

by the Lord,

so how can anyone understand

his own way?

(Proverbs 20:24 HCSB)

The goal is not to just get back to normal. This may be the reason He has allowed this difficult season: to mold you and shape you, to make you more dependent on Him than on a comfortable lifestyle or a checkbook. What is the next right step? You can be confident He wants to build you up not tear you down. When we're resistant to His direction, we're choosing to live by our terms, we'll end up with something less than what He has for us.

In Matthew 8, we read about the disciples in their boat going across to the other side of the lake when a "furious" storm overwhelmed the boat. The Disciples were afraid for their lives but Jesus slept through it. He may have been asleep but He was not unaware. They ran to Him for help and He calmed the storm. His question to them was, "You of little faith, why are you so afraid?" (8:26) They feared for their lives and probably did not want to go through a situation like that again. As awful as it was, did they learn to trust in Him more? He used the experience to shape their lives and strengthen their faith. Hopefully, their goal was not to just get back to normal. It may have been to get back to dry ground but following this, how could they just return to normal? They were amazed and saw Jesus differently, "What kind of man is this? Even the winds and the waves obey him!" (v.27).

Father, help me to know and do the next right thing. Rather than focus on everything going on around me, help me to focus on You, to trust that You are directing my steps, that You have a plan and a purpose in all of this, and that You will get me through this.

A Word of Hope for Today: He has not forgotten you. Your circumstances have not taken Him by surprise. The waves may be overtaking the boat but He is with You. Have faith, walk in faith.

Make out a list of five things you will do this week. Start doing them. Do the next right thing. Small steps. Don't get overwhelmed with the whole picture, focus on these five tasks, one at a time.

Day 30

Finally, brothers and sisters, whatever is true, whatever is noble, whatever is right, whatever is pure, whatever is lovely, whatever is admirable — if anything is excellent or praiseworthy — think about such things. Whatever you have learned or received or heard from me, or seen in me — put it into practice. And the God of peace will be with you. (Philippians 4:8, 9 NIV)

As we are transformed and our minds are renewed, we begin to think different. We see things differently. Our perceptions are more in line with His will and His character. He is shaping our character as well as calling us on our actions. More than just giving us a revised list of acceptable behavior, our thoughts undergo renovation also. He wants to change how we think.

Some people are just naturally glass-half-full kind of people. They see the good in others. They are hopeful about change. They give others the benefit of the doubt. Their first thought is not that something won't work out. They see new opportunities. Other people are more glass-half-empty. They see the problem before they see the solution. They already know their lives will be interrupted and inconvenienced. There is a possibility for good but they are expecting the worse. They can tell you all of the bad things that could happen. Most of them see themselves as positive (or realistic) because they know they aren't trying to be negative. But pessimism leaks out. They know change is possible they just doubt it will happen for them... or you... or anyone else.

you were taught... to be made new in the attitude of your minds
(Ephesians 4:23)

Regardless of our perspective, Paul instructs all of us to put our minds on those things that are true, noble, right, pure, lovely, admirable, excellent, and worthy of praise. Some versions use the term "dwell". Keep your mind on these things - not just think about them every so often, dwell on it.

If our thoughts and words are grounded in what is noble or pure, our conversations and relationships would be transformed. If our minds are fixed on what is true and admirable we may respond to others with more compassion and grace. We may see them in a different light.

Anxiety has a way of twisting our thoughts away from the truth. We begin to focus on things that haven't happened yet but we think we know how it will turn out. We dwell on worst-case scenarios with little or no consideration of how God fits into the equation. We play and replay events that happened or events that have never happened. These thoughts aren't grounded in faith or hope, just fear.

Then Paul has the audacity to tell us to think on things that are excellent and praiseworthy. *But he doesn't know what it's like living with... or how often* she... or what I've been through. He hasn't had to deal with cancer, depression, or abuse. He didn't grow up with an alcoholic, abusive... Paul had his own circumstances to overcome or work through. He had to come to terms with his haunting past of persecuting and killing believers, being threatened, accused and rejected by church leaders, being imprisoned for preaching the gospel, and wondering which prison term would end in death. His past wasn't pretty but God chose to use him.

Set your minds on things above, not on earthly things.
(Colossians 3:2 NIV)

He knew he didn't do things perfectly, but Paul encouraged the believers in Philippi to put into practice what they had learned from him or had seen in him. His life must have been a testimony to them. He was sitting in prison but this was not proof or evidence that God had abandoned him or he had done anything wrong. He was in prison but he was not focused on his circumstances. Paul rejoiced. He kept his thoughts on what was good and upright and praiseworthy. He encouraged them to live out the transformational message of the gospel that they had heard from him.

Do you have certain thought patterns that work against you? Do you label situations or people even before you get to know them? Do you think so concretely that you misinterpret harmless comments from others? Do you see things in stark all-or-nothing terms with no room for compromise or flexibility?

Do you focus so heavy on the problems you see in others then overlook or justify your own behavior? Are you so focused on proving others wrong that you overshadow their positive traits? Do you emotionally cut others off because of one offense? Do you argue with others regardless of what they are saying? Do you find fault in everything or everyone? Do you make judgments before you have heard all of the facts? Rather than gradual changes, do you flip-flop from one extreme to another? Do you dwell on situations or people so often that it interrupts your sleep, distracts you from other concerns, or keeps you from doing what needs to get done?

Paul explained to his readers that as they out into practice these teachings, the God of peace and the peace of God would be with them. The God of peace. The God who reconciles all things. The God who is able to bring all things in subjection to Himself. The God who works all things together for good. The God who brings order to the chaos and confusion.

There can be peace within when we recognize He is God. When we surrender to His will, we can keep our minds on those things that are good and pure and true rather than on what could or did happen, how it's not going to be ok, or what if... We can challenge those thoughts that are not in line with His will, which is good, acceptable, and perfect.

*Every good thing given
and every perfect gift is from above,
coming down from
the Father of lights,
with whom there is no variation
or shifting shadows.*
(James 1:17 NASB)

Father, every good and perfect gift comes from above, from You. I am secure in You. I commit to keep my thoughts on what is pleasing to You. Help me to challenge the thoughts that are negative, hurtful, self-defeating, and not in line with Your will or character. Today, help me to keep my thoughts on that which is true, noble, right, pure, lovely, admirable, excellent, and worthy of praise.

A Word of Hope for Today: let His peace rule over your heart today. As crisis hits or panic sets in, rest in His peace rather than allowing your mind to cycle through all of the bad that could happen. Let His peace calm you. As your mind wants to replay that hurtful experience, continue to put your mind on what is good and upright. Challenge the thoughts that you know what others are thinking or you know their motives. Remind yourself of who you are in Him.

Everyday for the next week, write out three positive things that you would not normally credit as positive. Find the good in something or someone and tell them.

Carry each other's burdens, and in this way you will fulfill the law of Christ. If anyone thinks they are something when they are not, they deceive themselves. Each one should test their own actions. Then they can take pride in themselves alone, without comparing themselves to someone else, for each one should carry their own load. Nevertheless, the one who receives instruction in the word should share all good things with their instructor. Do not be deceived: God cannot be mocked. A man reaps what he sows.

(*Galatians 6:2-7 NIV*)

There are at least 58 different "one another" passages in the New Testament. Love one another, forgive one another, live in peace with one another, serve one anther, greet one another with a holy kiss, etc... Even, carry one another's burdens (HCSB). We were made to live in community with *one another*. But, even in Christian community, we can lose our identity.

Increased anxiety or depression may be a product of not clearly defining our individuality or identity. We may get anxious, frustrated, or resentful when others cross our boundaries, when they invade our personal, emotional, relational, moral, or financial space. We feel depressed, taken advantage of, or overwhelmed when we live in a perpetual state of poorly defined and imbalanced boundary lines. Boundaries can be difficult to define because they are emotional and relational, not just physical.

We're called to love one another but we can still practice healthy boundaries, even as the Body of Christ. Boundaries don't have to be walls to keep others out. Boundaries are lines that define who we are and who we are not.

> Don't be deceived:
> God is not mocked.
> For whatever a man sows
> he will also reap
> (Galatians 6:7 HCSB)

We reap what we sow. I am responsible for me when I recognize these are my thoughts, my emotions, my actions, my choices, my mistakes, my... These are mine, if I take responsibility for these rather than trying to make everyone else responsible for how I feel or what I do. We have odd ways of expressing this. We say a lot of things like, "you make me mad" or "she made me hit her." As long as I think you make me mad, I don't change me, I change you. We yell, scream, accuse, shut down, pull away, use force, or make threats then the other person stops what they're doing and we feel better. Isn't that the way it's supposed to work?

When we take responsibility for ourselves, we recognize and own that this is our anger, our controlling behavior, our anxious self, our immaturity. Rather than blaming others, we own it and define who we are (the good and the ugly). Even our reactions to others should be our responsibility. This may sound like 'therapist talk' but no one "makes" us mad, these are our feelings, we allow ourselves to get angry. If we allow others to to control our emotions that much, it is a sign of emotional immaturity.

You may be blaming others for your anxiety or depression. You may blame them for your circumstances and how awful the situation is, but you have choices of what to do from this point on. They may have done things to hurt you and affect you, but how you react to that is up to you. You may blame your parents for doing all of the wrong things while you were growing up but at some point you grew up; your life and your choices became yours... if you'll own it.

For each person

will have to carry his own load.
(Galatians 6:5 HCSB)

Some of the pressure or stress we experience may be because we take responsibility for things or people that are not our responsibility. Rather than giving in to guilt or fear or emotional manipulation, can we allow others to feel or think or do what they are going to feel and think and do? Sometimes, it may not be caused by the other person, it may be our fear or anxiety that's driving our behavior or irrational thoughts. It may be our perception or assumptions that keeps us stressed or striving to please. Can we let others be responsible for themselves: for their emotions, their choices, their behavior, and their thoughts?

Can we be honest with ourselves? Most of us don't like when other people think we're wrong or think less of us. We avoid conflict. We please others. We think we have to convince them or change what they think or feel. Not our responsibility. Most of the time, they're adults, they are not our responsibility.

Therefore each of you
must put off falsehood and
speak truthfully to your neighbor,
for we are all members of one body.
(Ephesians 4:25)

When it gets too uncomfortable for us we think we have to change them. We change them to manage our emotions, to lower our anxiety. The lines between us become very unclear, who's responsible for who?

And we don't like feeling uncomfortable or anxious, we want to feel good. So we avoid conflict or difficult conversations or awkward situations or unwanted emotional reactions from others. We play it safe. We say things we don't mean, we commit to things we don't want to commit to, we carry the weight of the conflict, and we walk on eggshells. After all, isn't that better than someone getting angry at us or thinking less of us? We avoid awkward, unwanted feelings and then wonder why the relationship never really improves.

Can we be comfortable with being uncomfortable? Can we let others be upset or angry or disapproving or disappointed? Can we let them feel what they are going to feel and be ok with it? Rather than trying to please everyone all the time about everything, can we let our anxiety go up a little. Or a lot? Can we change our relationships by changing ourselves? Can I have a new me by Friday? Can we find our strength and security in our Heavenly Father?

Most of our unhealthy relational patterns come from pleasing others or pleasing ourselves. As believers, we can allow ourselves to be defined by our identity in Christ. Are we pleasing God or man?

We can help carry the burdens of others, not because we have to, but because we choose to. We can learn to give out of genuine love and concern, not because we feel guilty or obligated or afraid. Even with God, we don't give or love or worship out of fear or guilt but out of love. There should be choice. Jesus said if we love Him, we'll obey His commands. We choose Him, we choose to worship Him, to obey Him.

Therefore, as we have opportunity, let us do good to all people, especially to those who belong to the family of believers.
(Galatians 6:10 NIV)

We can allow those who need to carry their own load to carry it without us feeling like we're bad

Christians. Carrying one another's burdens doesn't mean we take all of their responsibility. It also means that we are free and available to help them because we are not already overwhelmed with a load pushed on us by someone else. We help them because they are wounded or hurt or struggling and God has freed us up to be there for them. He may be using our times of pain or comfort or healing to reach out to them in love.

Father, Help me to practice healthy boundaries with a loving and generous attitude. Help me to actively love others with a sense of joy, not out of fear or coercion or false guilt. Help me to be responsible with my emotions, my choices, my actions and to speak the truth in love.

A Word of Hope for Today: Perfect love casts out fear. You don't have to live afraid of what others may do or what they may think of you. Most of the worrying or dread about them will only affect you not them. You can't change them. You are responsible for you. There should be appropriate responsibility for those in your life you are responsible for (your children, a disabled loved one, an elderly parent). God wants us to give to others freely and generously. We can't do that when we are so overwhelmed with the burdens of others.

Examine your relationships. Are you carrying anxiety and stress because you are living in fear or constant state of anxiety? Take steps in each of those relationships to speak the truth in love.

Day 32

I keep asking that the God of our Lord Jesus Christ, the glorious Father, may give you the Spirit of wisdom and revelation, so that you may know him better. I pray that the eyes of your heart may be enlightened in order that you may know the hope to which he has called you, the riches of his glorious inheritance in his holy people, and his incomparably great power for us who believe.

(Ephesians 1:17–19a NIV)

Prayer remains one of our most powerful weapons. The apostle Paul included two of his prayers in his letter to the believers in Ephesus. He had helped establish this church and he was concerned for their spiritual wellbeing. He was praying that they would understand their identity and value in Christ.

In chapter one, Paul's prayer was for the believers to know God in a deeper way. He prayed that God would give them wisdom and revelation to make this possible. He prayed that their hearts would be open to the understanding of three things: the hope God was calling them to, the riches of what God places in His people, and the power that God's people have. All of this so that we might know Him better.

As a prisoner for the Lord, then,
I urge you to live a life worthy
of the calling you have received.
(Ephesians 4:1)

The letter to the Ephesians draws us over and over again to our identity in Christ. Paul used many phrases throughout chapter one to emphasize this: *"To God's holy people in Ephesus, the faithful in Christ Jesus* (v.1) *...who has blessed us in the heavenly realms with every spiritual blessing in Christ.* (v.3) *For He chose us in Him before the creation of the world to be holy and blameless in his sight.* (v.4) *In love He predestined us for adoption to sonship through Jesus Christ, in accordance with his pleasure and will* (v.5) *In Him we have redemption through His blood, the forgiveness of sins, in accordance with the riches of God's grace* (v.7) *that He lavished on us. With all wisdom and understanding,* (v.8) *He made known to us the mystery of His will according to his good pleasure, which He purposed in Christ,*(v.9) *In Him we were also chosen, having been predestined according to the plan of Him who works out everything in conformity with the purpose of his will, (v.11) in order that we, who were the first to put our hope in Christ, might be for the praise of his glory.* (v.12) *And you also were included in Christ when you heard the message of truth, the gospel of your salvation. When you believed, you were marked in him with a seal, the promised Holy Spirit, (v.13) who is a deposit guaranteeing our inheritance until the redemption of* *those who are God's possession—to the praise of his glory.* (v.14)

For God has not given us

a spirit of fearfulness,

but one of

power, love, and sound judgment.

(2 Timothy 1:7 HCSB)

Paul defined and described who we are in Christ. Our identity is secure and established. And then Paul transitioned into His first prayer – that these believers who are secure in Christ would know, in a more intimate way, the God who has redeemed them. Paul related to them who they were in Christ and he prayed that they would be able to fully grasp the meaning. More than just knowledge about God, he prayed that the eyes of their hearts would be opened to this truth, that they would know the hope they have in Christ, the fullness of what God has placed in His people, and the power they possess. This is almost a contradiction – he prayed that they would comprehend this power that is "incomparably great", the "exceeding greatness of His power "(KJV).

And then he described that power: the same power and the same Spirit that raised Jesus from the dead, the same power that exalted Him above all authority and power. There is no other power like it and He has placed this power in each of us. He prayed that they would have the wisdom and discernment to see and know they have this active, living, transformational power within them. The power that is above all authority and power.

Anxiety and depression have power. They can influence how we feel, what we do, how we think, and how we react. They can overpower us emotionally, physically, mentally, and relationally. They can leave us feeling defeated spiritually. Anxiety has the power to twist our thoughts, drain our energy, leave us stagnate, relationally isolate us, and spiritually decapitate us. Paul prayed the believers in Ephesus would have a firm grasp of God's power, regardless of what they might have been facing. We read more in chapter three:

"For this reason I kneel before the Father, from whom every family in heaven and on earth derives its name. I pray that out of his glorious riches he may strengthen you with power through his Spirit in your inner being, so that Christ may dwell in your hearts through faith. And I pray that you, being rooted and established in love, may have power, together with all the Lord's holy people, to grasp how wide and long and high and deep is the love of Christ, and to know this love that surpasses knowledge — that you may be filled to the measure of all the fullness of God. Now to him who is able to do immeasurably more than all we ask or imagine, according to his power that is at work within us, to him be glory in the church and in Christ Jesus throughout all

generations, for ever and ever! Amen."

(Ephesians 3:14-21 NIV)

God's power is not magic. It is the power of His strength in us. It is the power to know Him in all of His fullness. It is the power to know and be convinced of the depth and fullness of His love. It is His Spirit in our inner being empowering Christ to dwell inside of us. It is His Spirit and His power enabling us to live out *all* that He is doing in us. It is being filled "to the measure of all the fullness of God". And this is all accomplished by "His power that is at work within us". His power, which is "able to do immeasurably more than all we ask or imagine". Paul prayed for believers to fully comprehend and utilize this power. It is no accident He included his prayers in his letters. He wanted the believers in Ephesus to know how fervently he was praying and what he was praying.

Paul's prayers are grounded in the clear understanding of our identity in Christ. He was not just praying for us to have a nice day or a blessed meal but to be fully embraced, empowered, and enveloped with the Spirit of God within us. Throughout this letter, he identified who we are in Christ. He prayed for us to know the richness and completeness of what God has done in us and for us.

Faith is not a magic pill to make everything go away. It is our belief that the God living inside of us is completing the work He began in us. It is the knowledge of who He is and believing He will do what He says. It is accepting and living the truth that He is transforming us. From the inside out. He is empowering us. Through the strength of His strength.

He loves us and wants what is good and immeasurably more than what we want for ourselves.

Heavenly Father, I pray that out of Your glorious riches, You would strengthen us with Your might through Your Spirit deep in the core of who we are, so that Christ would dwell mightily in our hearts. That, being rooted and grounded in love, we would have power, together with all believers to grasp how powerful, how extravagant, and how immense the love of Christ is. Father, help us to know and live this love that surpasses knowledge – that we would be filled to the measure of all the fullness of You. You are able and desire to do so much more than all we ask or imagine through Your power that is at work within us. To You be glory throughout all generations, for ever and ever! Amen

A Word of Hope for Today: Whatever you are facing today, He wants to be with you through it all. You may feel defeated and exhausted but He will give you the strength to keep going. You may feel alone or void of all hope but He wants to encourage you. He wants you to know the fullness of His power within you, to know the hope He is calling you to, to know and experience the vastness of His unfailing love.

Identify and challenge the thoughts that tell you He is not enough, that He does not care, that you are defeated, or that nothing will change. Challenge those anxious, despondent thoughts. Confront the feelings that are working against you. Commit to not let these feelings control your thoughts or actions.

What is one thing you can do today that you would not normally do because of anxiety or depression? Break it down into small steps and start taking the first step. Don't get distracted or discouraged by looking at the whole picture, just take the first step. Tell yourself to get up. Don't see yourself out walking on the road, stand up. Then put on your shoes...

Day 33

This you know, my beloved brethren. But everyone must be quick to hear, slow to speak and slow to anger; for the anger of man does not achieve the righteousness of God.

(James 1:19, 20 NASB)

Be angry, and yet do not sin; do not let the sun go down on your anger, and do not give the devil an opportunity.

(Ephesians 4:26, 27 NASB)

A man's discretion makes him slow to anger, And it is his glory to overlook a transgression.

(Proverbs 19:11 NASB)

A hot-tempered man stirs up conflict, but a man slow to anger calms strife.

(Proverbs 15:18 HCSB)

Irritability goes hand in hand with anxiety and depression. It's easy to get frustrated with the little things when everything else is already weighing on you. It feels like you're on your last nerve where everyone has already pushed too far and demanded too much. And, the smallest things can't seem to go right. The pieces just don't fit even when they are supposed to.

It's a clear symptom of anxiety or depression and it "snowballs". The more depressed or anxious we feel, the more irritable we are; the more irritable we are, the more anxious and depressed we feel. It feeds the fire. Letting these frustrations erupt will not resolve the real issues but sometimes it feels good to let off steam. Often though, we take it out on the wrong person at the wrong time for the wrong reason. *And then we blame them for what we did.*

A fool gives full vent to his anger,
but a wise man holds it in check.
(Proverbs 29:11 HCSB)

Anger is the easiest emotion to express, we don't even have to use words: We give a look, through down a book, walk away, huff and puff. They get the message. They may not know why we're mad but they know we're mad. It's so much easier than expressing love. It's easy to show love to those who love us, especially when everything is going perfect. It can be difficult to love those who are not loving towards us. Anger is easy.

Anger can be powerful. Expressing hurt or fear or rejection can make us feel vulnerable while expressing anger comes across strong. It's self-protection mode, our natural defense system. Anger can hurt others because they have hurt us (or, at least, we perceive hurt). It keeps us from being exposed or getting hurt again. It sends the message that we don't like what they did. Or, we don't like what we're feeling in that moment. It can be a knee-jerk reaction to keep us safe.

He who is slow to anger
is better than the mighty,
And he who rules his spirit,
than he who captures a city.
(Proverbs 16:32 NASB)

Our expectations, conscious and subconscious, spoken and un-spoken, may be at the root of this irritability. We have expectations of how we are supposed to be treated, how we're to be thought of, what others are supposed to do, think, or feel, how life is supposed to be, or when things are supposed to happen or not happen. The bucket is already full and we get upset when someone else or something else kicks the spigot back on. Sometimes, the spigot has been running wide-open for so long, we're not even sure it can be turned off. We've given up trying to empty out the bucket.

Some of these self-imposed expectations are not rational but, more than that, they are not in line with God's expectations. They are *our* rules for living that others are not mandated to adhere to. For some reason, others may not recognize our role as the center of the universe, the supreme boss. And they probably have their own set of rules that we don't adhere to. Their lists of expectations don't seem to fit into our busy lives. Maybe next time.

These expectations may be irrational because they are extreme, centered around us, absolutes, or centered around things or people that are not my responsibility. It's not very rational to think I should be able to rule their lives. Especially when I resist them intruding in mine. Sometimes these expectations are just not in line with God's Word, God's will, or God's way of doing things. I'm the one out of line so why am I irritated when they cross my boundaries?

A gentle answer turns away anger,
but a harsh word stirs up wrath.
(Proverbs 15:1 HCSB)

It doesn't mean that we don't still feel irritable, frustrated, taken advantage of, or ignored. It still hurts. But, it probably also sets us up for increased stress or disappointment. Irritability increases our sensitivity to sounds, conflict, personal space, responsibility, or crowded places. Our irritable reactions usually set others up to react just as harshly to us – getting us more of what we don't want.

James chapter one encourages us to be quick to listen, slow to speak, and slow to anger. Irritability increases with anxiety but it is still our responsibility in how we react. The feelings are there but we can control the behavior. Irritability may drive others away or lead them to feel criticized, belittled, or attacked.

Fools show their annoyance at once,
but the prudent overlook an insult.
(Proverbs 12:16 NIV)

When we have those reactions, we can apologize and be intentional to reconnect with others. We can also challenge the thoughts that tell us everything is supposed to be easy, good, or fair. We can challenge the thoughts that kick in when we feel attacked or criticized. We can recognize that most of the time when we are irritable we just don't want to be bothered with other people, we take it as an invasion or an intrusion. God is using some of these intrusions to shape us. It may be part of His plan even if it's not part of our plan.

We can challenge the thoughts or expectations that are not in line with God's word: difficult times will come, life is not fair and not supposed to be, we are supposed to give generously of our time and resources to others, we can overlook transgressions done towards us.

Many proverbs address anger. They are statements that indicate we have a choice in how we react. We may feel angry or irritated but we have a choice in what we do. It also helps to recognize the correlation between our anxiety level and our rush to react strongly to others.

> Refrain from anger
> and give up your rage;
> do not be agitated —
> it can only bring harm.
> (Psalms 37:8 HCSB)

Father, help me to control these emotions and irrational thoughts. Help me to be honest about why I am annoyed or irritable. Help me to speak the truth in love and to react with a servant's heart. Help me to be aware of how my words and actions affect or hurt others. Help me to keep my heart and mind on your kingdom, not mine.

A Word of Hope for Today: Your Heavenly Father knows you are human. He created you, He knows you have human tendencies. Let Him be your strength, your hope, your peace. When life is crashing in, take refuge in Him. Tell Him your frustrations and fears and worries but also let Him transform those anxious feelings. Let Him renew your mind and thoughts. Love one another deeply.

If there is someone you are consistently irritated or frustrated with, be intentional to treat them with love and compassion. Be honest and work through any hard feelings that may be there. Keep short accounts rather than letting all of it pile up. Apologize when you need to.

If it feels like your "bucket" is overflowing and there seems to be no relief in sight, talk to a pastor or trusted friend. Allow yourself to relax and be human. Be honest with yourself if your life is too complicated, too hectic, or out of balance. Seek out a counselor. Spend time in prayer and the Word. Be honest about the changes that need to happen and make the changes.

Day 34

Therefore, prepare your minds for action, keep sober in spirit, fix your hope completely on the grace to be brought to you at the revelation of Jesus Christ. As obedient children, do not be conformed to the former lusts which were yours in your ignorance, but like the Holy One who called you, be holy yourselves also in all your behavior; because it is written, "YOU SHALL BE HOLY, FOR I AM HOLY."   1 Peter 1:13-16 (NASB)

Holiness. God is holy. Being whole, complete, perfect, lacking nothing, and not an overabundance of anything. He is exactly who He is. "I am that I am". He is a holy God, set apart from His creation and needs nothing from us to be complete. He is not transforming or growing or becoming more of who He is supposed to be, He already is. Being holy, all of His attributes are complete and holy.

God is love. His love is holy. He cannot love with anything less than genuine perfect love. He's not sitting in Heaven wishing He was more caring or compassionate. He's not regretting that he blessed someone too much and didn't do enough for someone else. Thank God, His love for us is based on Him and not us. We don't have to earn it, we cannot earn it, and we don't deserve it. There is nothing we can do to make Him love us more and nothing we can do that He would love us less. His love for us is perfect, complete, holy.

God is good. His goodness is innate. He didn't become good or learn how to be good. He is not good because He has not messed up yet and when He does He will cease being good. He would also then cease being God. His goodness is not relative. He is not good just because He is a little bit better than someone else. His goodness is not subjective to us. He is good; He is the standard. Our understanding of good is relative to Him. Because He is good, He can have nothing to do with evil, sin. He is set apart from evil.

Because of His holiness, we can trust Him to always act in line with His character. We can trust Him to love us with an everlasting love and to only do what is in our genuine best interests. We can trust Him to be good. He can't lie, cheat, or steal. He can't tell us He is someone He is not. Our "genuine best interests" are based on ultimate good rather than what feels good or what we deem to be good. This is why He is also just. He cannot overlook our sin or depravity. He cannot overlook what we do just because we didn't mean to sin but did. His justice and love and goodness are in perfect balance.

So what does this have to do with my emotional struggles? He doesn't experience extreme mood swings or debilitating anxiety or dark days when He can't get out of bed. His emotions - anger, patience, happiness, joy, excitement, and jealousy - are all in perfect balance and in the perfect amount expressed at just the right time in the perfect way. Does He ever have a bad day? A bad year?

But just as he who called you
is holy,
so be holy in all you do;
for it is written:
"Be holy, because I am holy."
(1 Peter 1:15, 16 NIV)

He calls us to holiness. We are not whole, complete, righteous, perfect, or set apart on our own. God commanded us to be holy and then He made a way for it to happen. Sin is a reality, it separates us from God. He loves us, but the relationship was broken, severed because of sin. Jesus, holy and righteous, died for our sins and restored that relationship. In Him, we are made righteous, holy. *"He made Him who knew no sin to be sin on our behalf, so that we might become the righteousness of God in Him."* (2 Cor 5:21 NASB)

We are made holy, whole, complete, perfected. Salvation is more than just a get-out-of-jail-free card. More than just not going to hell or a free ticket into Heaven, we are redeemed, restored, healed, made new, and given new life; we are transformed. The debt we owed is no longer owed, it was paid. The eternal separation that was there between us and God was removed, we are reconciled back to the Father. The power of sin and death were defeated, we are empowered by the Spirit of God alive in us. And then He tells us, "be holy as I am holy". He redeems us, restores us, and transforms us and calls us to live out what He has done in us.

"knowing that you were not redeemed with perishable things like silver or gold from your futile way of life inherited from your forefathers, but with precious blood, as of a lamb unblemished and spotless, the blood of Christ. For He was foreknown before the foundation of the world, but has appeared in these last times for the sake of you who through Him are believers in God, who raised Him from the dead and gave Him glory, so that your faith and hope are in God.

(1 Peter 1:18-21 NASB)

So what does this have to do with my emotional struggles? He has equipped us and empowered us to deal with what we face, real or perceived. He has not set us up for failure. He cannot lie. He is not plotting against us. He wants us to see ourselves as He sees us. He wants us to recognize our identity in Him. He knows who He says we are and what He says we are capable of. This is not the "have more faith and your anxiety will go away" speech. This is the "trust in His character and holiness to empower and equip you to know Him more fully" speech. Don't do more so you'll be okay; trust He has and is doing His work in you. His goal is to make you holy not happy: to sanctify and transform your mind, to renew your spirit, to empower your hope and faith, to put into action what He is doing in you, and, above everything else, for you to know Him intimately and fully with no hindrances in the way.

*Pursue peace with everyone,
and holiness —
without it no one will see the Lord.*
(Hebrews 12: 14 HCSB)

Holy God, You redeemed me and reconciled me back to You. I am Yours. Don't let me get in the way of the work You are doing in me. Don't let me settle for less when You have so much more. Don't let me settle for good or nice or polite but to live holy and set apart for You. Show Yourself strong. I surrender my struggles and weaknesses. Take these anxious thoughts, this depressed spirit, this broken wounded heart, this weakened body, these hurtful or hurting relationships, and breathe new life into me. Help me to live to the fullest extent in You, to be holy as You are holy.

A Word of Hope for Today: God, the Creator of the universe, says you are precious in His sight. He is doing a work in you. He has redeemed you and given you purpose. You may not be able see all that now but your part is to believe and live like it's true.

No one can know how you see yourself. Be honest about how you think of yourself. Admit the wounds and the flaws. Confess the sin. On a piece of paper, draw a line down the middle. On the left side, write out what you think of you, good and bad. Write out what you tell yourself about you. On the right side, write out what God says about you. Don't just skip this assignment because you "already know what He thinks" about you. Write it out. His word is truth. This is who He says you are. This is what He is working in you. Focus on the rights side of the paper. Challenge what is written on the left side with His word, His truth.

Day 35

Not that I speak from want, for I have learned to be content in whatever circumstances I am.

Philippians 4:11 (NASB)

He asked me to speak for him at his high school graduation. It was a small Christian school and each of the 12 graduates had a staff member speak a few words about the graduate. I was also leading a few worship songs in the graduation ceremony; praise and worship songs picked by the graduates. When I asked what song he chose, his response was, "whatever", he didn't care.

During the weeks leading up to graduation, his response was always the same when I asked about his song choice, "whatever". During the ceremony, when it was my turn to speak for the young man, I explained that he had chosen "whatever". I then sat at the keyboard and banged out whatever clashing, dissonant cacophony my hands happened to hit. After about 30 seconds of discordant whatever, I ended the "piece" with a few calming chords in the key of D and then resolved it with a Dmaj7. Ending on the root chord brought a sense of peace and resolve in spite of the clamor of dissonance before it. Out of the chaos came calm. It opened up the opportunity to share how a strong foundation and returning to our source of hope can provide the peace and resolve we are looking for rather than just going with whatever. The young man thought it was great but I may have crossed a line in trying to be funny but poignant.

We have to he prepared for whatever but not just go with whatever happens or whatever others are doing. The apostle Paul tells us, *"Not that I speak from want, for I have learned to be content in whatever circumstances I am."* (Philippians 4:11 NASB). We can't always control what happens but we can control how we react to it. Paul faced a variety of conflicts, obstacles, crisis, and disruptions. Missionary journeys, church planting, letter writing, training young pastors, public debates, building up the Body of Christ, he was a busy man. Then throw on top of that - prison, journeys to Rome, and ship wrecks. He had to deal with whatever came his way. *"For when we came into Macedonia, we had no rest, but we were harassed at every turn—conflicts on the outside, fears within. But God, who comforts the downcast, comforted us by the coming of Titus"* (2 Corinthians 7:5,6 NIV). Conflicts on the outside, fears on the inside, downcast, and depressed, but he was ready for whatever.

That is why, for Christ's sake,
I delight in weaknesses, in insults,
in hardships, in persecutions,
in difficulties.
For when I am weak,
then I am strong.
(2 Corinthians 12:10 NIV)

Paul's strength and readiness were rooted in Christ. He knew who he was in Christ and who Christ was in him. How do we find the strength and endurance to press through and overcome whatever is coming against us?

Prosperity preaching wants us to believe we can name it and claim it, we control what happens, God does our bidding according to our wills, or we can just change whatever it is we don't like or what we want to avoid. Paul gives us a different perspective. He believed he could do all things through Christ who was his strength. He learned to be content in the middle of unfortunate circumstances. He learned to be comforted by God as he pursued after God's will. His joy and peace and contentment were not dependent on convincing God to give in to his every desire. It was his desire to give into God's authority and power. *"But he said to me, 'My grace is sufficient for you, for my power is made perfect in weakness.' Therefore I will boast all the more gladly about my weaknesses, so that Christ's power may rest on me."* (2 Corinthians 12:9 NIV). Can we be so submitted to His will that we are willing to face whatever He allows us to face?

God does answer prayer but in His name, according to His will, when we ask in faith believing in His ability, not ours. Jesus made several "whatever" statements also.

Whatever you ask in My name, that will I do, so that the Father may be glorified in the Son.

(John 14:13 NASB)

If you abide in Me, and My words abide in you, ask whatever you wish, and it will be done for you.

(John 15:7 NASB)

You did not choose Me but I chose you, and appointed you that you would go and bear fruit, and that your fruit would remain, so that whatever you ask of the Father in My name He may give to you.

(John 15:16 NASB)

But when He, the Spirit of truth, comes, He will guide you into all the truth; for He will not speak on His own initiative, but whatever He hears, He will speak; and He will disclose to you what is to come.

(John 16:13 NASB)

There is a dependency on Christ through all of these verses. There is a higher purpose than just our happiness or comfort. It is for God the Father to be glorified. It is the result of us abiding in Him. It is to bear fruit and impact those around us. It is to be led and directed by Him rather than our roller-coaster emotions. When we endure and persevere in His name and in His strength we are empowered and He is glorified. Whatever we do is for His glory as we trust in His goodness and His strength.

Whatever you do in word or deed, do all in the name of the Lord Jesus, giving thanks through Him to God the Father.

(Colossians 3:17 NASB)

So whether you eat or drink or whatever you do, do it all for the glory of God.

(1 Corinthians 10:31 NIV)

If there is unrest, anxiety, or hopelessness controlling your heart, continue to bring it to God in prayer. Pray according to His word, His promises. Accept that His will may be different than yours. Press on faithfully. When you feel the answer is "no", continue to trust that He is good, that if He will not take it away, He will empower you to get through it. This may not be what you want to hear but when we are weak He is strong. We find our strength in His strength.

Father, help me to be content in You. Whatever my circumstances, help me to find joy and peace and strength in You. Replace the fear and dread with Your peace, take away the discouragement and replace it with your joy. You are my strength when I am weak.

A Word of Hope for Today: He heals the brokenhearted and comforts the downcast. Cast your cares on Him because He cares for you. It's ok to let the pain show. One step at a time, one day at a time, one moment at a time, continue to bring it to Him in prayer. Abide in Him. Let His words abide in you. Jesus told us to pray in His name, as we abide in Him. His response to your prayers may be to continue to give you hope and strength and joy and peace even when your circumstances say it should not be there.

"...whatever is true, whatever is noble, whatever is right, whatever is pure, whatever is lovely, whatever is admirable—if anything is excellent or praiseworthy—think about such things. Whatever you have learned or received or heard from me, or seen in me—put it into practice. And the God of peace will be with you."   (Philippians 4:8, 9 NIV)

Day 36

"Ask and it will be given to you; seek and you will find; knock and the door will be opened to you. For everyone who asks receives; the one who seeks finds; and to the one who knocks, the door will be opened.

Which of you, if your son asks for bread, will give him a stone? Or if he asks for a fish, will give him a snake? If you, then, though you are evil, know how to give good gifts to your children, how much more will your Father in heaven give good gifts to those who ask him!"

(Matthew 7:7-11 NIV)

You could hear it in her voice. The pain was visible on her face. She didn't even try to hide it. She was bitter and hurt and God was to blame. Long ago, she arrived at the place where she stopped believing. Not just a detour in her faith or church attendance; she stopped believing *in* Him. God was real, He existed; her hatred was proof of that. She stopped trusting when she stopped believing He was good.

It became too easy to explain everything with a tidy Christian label. *Bad things happen so we'll "grow stronger". He didn't cause it but He allowed it. We can't understand - His ways are higher than ours. We grow spiritually through adversity. We need the valleys to appreciate the mountaintops. He has a plan for our lives. We have to accept it by faith.*

When we get to Heaven, we'll understand. Sometimes His answer is 'no'. He works all things together for our good. God knew something worse was going to happen. God needed them in Heaven more than...

She knew there was truth in some of these answers and, in the past, they carried her through many difficult struggles but at some point they stopped being enough. Bad things happened. Tragedies hit. Relationships exploded. Trusted loved ones left or died or worse. Misery set in. But God still came out the good guy. Looking like the hero. Smelling like a rose. She learned to hate roses. Bad things happened and He was still labeled good. Even when the bad outweighed the good.

She had lived a life of faith. Had been active in her church. Had prayed with others and led small groups. She was faithful when others seemed to wander. She gave generously and shared her faith with others. She had even shared those tidy little explanations with those who were grieving or wounded. And she believed it. Every word of it. She knew her God was faithful. Even when their circumstances were insurmountable, she was the strong voice of encouragement and hope that convinced them to go on. And then one day...

It was too much to bear. Most things she could make sense of but not this. In the past, her mind could see or at least comprehend the good that could come out of tragedies. Her heart could accept that some things had to be believed by faith. Her mind could grasp that there were many things she did not know. She could admit she didn't have to understand something for it to be good. *But some things cannot be labeled good when they are not.*

We bleed when we're cut. We cry when we're hurt. We grieve when we've lost. And time keeps moving forward whether we accept to go on with it or not. Our acceptance doesn't make it true or not. We don't have that kind of power. Sometimes we think we do or we wish we did.

" Give us this day our daily bread."

(Matthew 6:11 NASB)

Jesus taught His disciples how to pray, "Our Father, who art in Heaven, hallowed be thy name. Thy kingdom come, Thy will done on earth as it is in Heaven. Give us this day our daily bread. Forgive us our trespasses as we forgive those who trespass against us. And lead us not into temptation but deliver us from evil. For Thine is the kingdom and the power and the glory forever.". (Mt. 6:9-13)

There was a clear distinction of whose kingdom, whose *will* ruled. Jesus clearly defined God as holy (hallowed) and somewhere up in Heaven. He is set apart from man. Above man. But Jesus also interwove this idea of a Holy, set apart God with a new perspective of God as "our Father". Not just His Father, the father of Jesus the only begotten Son of God, but "our" Father. The Old Testament understanding of God was a God, high and holy, the God of our Fathers, the Lord God Almighty, the God of Abraham, Isaac, and Jacob. Jesus taught them to relate to this Father in prayer, talk to Him.

"Which of you,
if your son asks for bread,
will give him a stone?"
(Matthew 7:9)

Throughout the Sermon on the Mount, Jesus taught on prayer, forgiveness, faith, giving, fasting, and tithing. He taught them how to pray, what to pray, and to be persistent in prayer. In Matthew 7, He taught them to keep asking, keep seeking, keep knocking. And then He explained that we can expect good from God our Father. *"Which of you, if your son asks for bread, will give him a stone? Or if he asks for a fish, will give him a snake? If you, then, though you are evil, know how to give good gifts to your children, how much more will your Father in heaven give good gifts to those who ask him!"* (Matthew 7:9-11 NIV)

He taught them to pray, "give us this day our daily bread..." and then a moment later He used the example of children asking their father for bread. He used an example they all could relate to. As fathers, they knew they wanted good things for their children. He didn't beat around the bush and say some were good fathers and some were bad. He faced them head on, "If you then, being evil, know how to give good gifts to your children, how much more will your Father who is in heaven give what is good to those who ask Him!" (NASB)

Sometimes we define good and evil by our experiences, through our emotions, or by popular opinion. Jesus defined good in relation to a Holy

God, "there is none good but God." (Mt 19:17, Mk 10:18, Lk 18:19). The men standing around Him probably would have shared that same perspective. Especially, in this context, they would have agreed, how much more would a holy God do only what is right and good.

Not only do we interpret good and evil through our experiences or emotions, but then we may begin to label God through those same standards. If He gives us bad gifts, He must not be a good God. Sometimes what we call a serpent, He knows it to be a fish. Or, we think we are asking for a piece of bread but He knows it to be a rock. We get frustrated or disappointed when it turns out different than what we want. But if He gives us a snake just because we want it or ask for it, He would be a bad father. Sometimes rocks look awfully tempting and we want it bad enough to go around our Heavenly Father. Can we trust in His character? Can we trust Him to give us what is good? Can we believe that He loves us with a pure love and He cannot do evil towards us?

...for God is greater than our heart and knows all things.
(1 John 4:20b NASB)

Sometimes the crisis we are going through is so traumatic, the only answers our experiences and emotions and intrusive thoughts tell us is that it is too much, too little, too late: there is no good in this. God must be evil to cause it or even allow it. Even if He walks with us through this, we don't want to go through it. The situation is dreadful. He is not good.

As awful as the situation may be, we are still interpreting it through our temporal, battered, emotional, self-centric finite view. We determine He is not good based on our feelings and the reality we're trying to avoid. Not the most objective or accurate way to judge an eternal, infinite supreme being and His character. It's like saying the band was awful because you sat in the nose-bleed section and the guy sitting beside you wouldn't stop talking.

He is an all-powerful, all-knowing being who cannot go against His character. Being holy, He is complete and whole, lacking in nothing, which means He is light and in Him there is no darkness, He is love and cannot act other than in genuine compassion towards us, and He is good so what He has for us is only what is in our ultimate best interest. And, because He is God, His world does not revolve around us. Our lives were meant to revolve around Him, He is the center. Rather than trying to make sense of why He does not fit into our plans, we have to recognize life and meaning and God will only make sense with Him as the center.

See what great love
the Father has lavished on us,
that we should be called children
of God! And that is what we are!
(1 John 3:1 NASB)

Father, give us this day our daily bread. Give us what we need. Help me to trust You are good and You are more than enough for what I am going through. Sometimes, the pain or the conditions seem unbearable or unmanageable. I can be honest with You about my struggle, my lack of faith or trust. I don't always understand why You allow so much pain or difficulty. I have to believe You are greater than whatever I face. You are faithful. You are good.

A Word of Hope for Today: A simple story about a dad giving his son a piece of bread will not explain away the injustice or devastation you're feeling. It may not help you see Him as good. It may help to understand that if He is who He says He is, He is the ultimate source of life and power and good in the universe and is not limited or defined by your circumstances. He has promised to be with you through whatever it is you are going through. Rather than letting the crisis and pain defeat you and define God, allow Him to empower you and redefine the crisis. The pain is there whether you believe in Him or not.

Therefore, since we have so great a cloud of witnesses surrounding us, let us also lay aside every encumbrance and the sin which so easily entangles us, and let us run with endurance the race that is set before us, fixing our eyes on Jesus, the author and perfecter of faith, who for the joy set before Him endured the cross, despising the shame, and has sat down at the right hand of the throne of God. For consider Him who has endured such hostility by sinners against Himself, so that you will not grow weary and lose heart. (Hebrews 12:1-3 NASB)

We all need a cheer squad, a support team, to encourage us and keep us going. We need to hear it is ok to hope. We need to hear we will make it through. In spite of us, God has not given up on us. In spite of our circumstances, we can press on. Paul stated with confidence the course ahead of us, "and let us run with endurance the race that is set before us." He doesn't question that we can or should keep on going.

Long distance runners have a different strategy than the sprinter. The marathon runner doesn't use up all of his strength sprinting off of the starting line, he knows there is a long journey ahead of him. But he also trains different. He prepares for long distances by running long distances. He builds the muscles and the stamina he will use in the race. And, unless there is an injury, he is consistently preparing for the race. The sprinter has a specific set of skills as well. He wants to cover the measured distance in the shortest time possible. He pushes his body and his muscles to the extreme. He trains his body and muscles for those short explosions of energy. The race may be over in 11 seconds but the sprinter is constantly training with that 100 meters in mind.

Our race is a race of endurance not a sprint. Sometimes the race lasts years not hours or seconds. When the course is difficult and uphill, the going gets rough and the pace can slow down. That's when the cheerleaders can be helpful. Standing on the sideline cheering us on, passing out water as we run (or walk) by, and sometimes coming along side us to run with us. We were meant to run together.

Therefore encourage one another and build up one another, just as you also are doing.
(1 Thessalonians 5:11 NASB)

We need the encouragement. We're commanded in scripture to encourage one another. God didn't intend for us to run the race alone. *"Let us hold fast the confession of our hope without wavering, for He who promised is faithful; and let us consider how to stimulate one another to love and good deeds, not forsaking our own assembling together, as is the habit of some, but encouraging one another; and all the more as you see the day drawing near."*

(Hebrews 10:23-25 NASB) We need to know that others are supporting us and believe in us. It helps to know that others have gone through similar or worse trials than us and they are still going. They survived and so will we.

Depression can lead to isolation. Seeing others happy is not always an encouragement, it can be a reminder of how unhappy we are. At times, being around others can feed those unsettling feelings of being alone, misunderstood, or mistreated. Others may be quick to tell us how to "fix" the problem or to point out everything we are doing wrong. But we were created to be in community, in relationship with others. It is an encouragement to find those who will listen or just be there. We are strengthened by the ones who let us know that they are thinking about us and praying for us, without judging us. They are the cheerleaders, the encouragers. They are the ones it is safe to open up to and to share our real thoughts and feelings.

But encourage one another daily,
as long as it is called "Today,"
so that none of you may be
hardened by sin's deceitfulness.
(Hebrews 3:13)

In bicycle racing, the cyclists form a tight group called a peloton as they're riding. This reduces drag and conserves energy for the cyclists on the inside of the pack. Each cyclist takes a turn on the outside or front blocking the brunt of headwind for the rest of the group. There's safety in numbers. They are still competing against one another but they are also working together to finish the race well. Rather than feeding into the patterns of depression, connecting with others who care and understand can be a healthy step. We often think it shows weakness but reaching out to others can be a healthy sign of faith.

"Do you not know that those who run in a race all run, but only one receives the prize? Run in such a way that you may win. Everyone who competes in the games exercises self-control in all things. They then do it to receive a perishable wreath, but we an imperishable Therefore I run in such a way, as not without aim; I box in such a way, as not beating the air; but I discipline my body and make it my slave, so that, after I have preached to others, I myself will not be disqualified."

(1 Corinthians 9:24-27 NASB)

All of the "heroes" we read about in scripture went through difficult times. They endured through deserts, wars, attacks, challenges to their faith, delayed answers to promises, devastating famines, intimidating giants, hungry lions, overwhelming odds, and massive armies. They endured. They stood strong when everything seemed to be working against them. We hear of God moving in their lives. This is who the author of Hebrews described when he tells us "we have so great a cloud of witnesses surrounding us." He wasn't referring to believers who never faced any problems but ones who overcame incredible circumstances. Our strength is not in our abilities but in the God who empowers us. This is why James tells us *"that the testing of your faith produces endurance. And let endurance have its perfect result, so that you may be perfect and complete, lacking in nothing."* (James 1:3,4 NASB) We build endurance for the race by staying in the race. We press on. Jesus endured the cross so that we could run with endurance and power rather than in defeat or emptiness.

For consider Him
who has endured such hostility
by sinners against Himself,
so that you will not grow weary
and lose heart.
(Hebrews 12:3 NASB)

Father, thank You for the strength to go on. Help me to keep my eyes on You and to not give up. Help me to be faithful to encourage others and build them up. Help me to hear their hurt or struggles and to speak words of hope and life. Help me to be open with my brothers and sisters in the faith and to faithfully share all that You are doing in my life.

A Word of Hope for Today: Your Heavenly Father is equipping you and empowering you to do all that He is calling you to do. He wants to see you thrive in Him. He is glorified as you endure and grow stronger and more like Him. He never intended for you to go through this all alone.

Challenge the thoughts that say you are supposed to do it on your own. If you are already connecting with others who encourage you and you encourage them, keep running the race together. If you're afraid others may not understand or will think less of you, take a step. Think of one or two people within your social group or community who would be safe to reach out to. Call them up this week and ask to just get together and talk.

Challenge the thoughts that say you are supposed to do it on your own. Be honest about the fear or pride that says you can't be transparent. If there is a deeper past issue that keeps you locked in and others locked out, talk to a pastor or counselor. Make the decision to not let those thoughts steal your joy or cloud over your days. Talk about the hidden secrets or personal rules that keep you gasping for breath or too wounded to run the race.

Day 38

One of the teachers of the law came and heard them debating. Noticing that Jesus had given them a good answer, he asked him, "Of all the commandments, which is the most important?"

"The most important one," answered Jesus, "is this: 'Hear, O Israel: The Lord our God, the Lord is one. Love the Lord your God with all your heart and with all your soul and with all your mind and with all your strength.' The second is this: 'Love your neighbor as yourself.' There is no commandment greater than these."

Mark 12:28-31

Priorities. First things first. Our checkbooks and our calendars are usually an accurate gauge for what is most important to us. It's easy to think that we have the right priorities but how we spend our time and our money indicate where our heart really is.

A crisis automatically becomes a priority when it hits. It becomes our primary focus. The bigger the crisis, the bigger the focus. And, usually, "our" crisis is more of a priority to us than someone else's crisis. We care about others and are concerned when they go through traumatic events but then we get distracted with our lives again. When we're not the one in the crisis, life goes on.

But crisis is the exception. Everyday life has a different set of rules when we are not in crisis. We occupy our time with what is important to us. Or, what feels good to us. We may want some things to be important but we build our lives around what is genuinely valued by us or what has leverage on us.

Jesus was asked what was the most important commandment. Of all that God, the creator of everything, instructs us to do, what is the most important thing to do? Jesus' response was to quote the Sh'ma Yisrael: "Hear, O Israel, the Lord our God, the Lord is one. Love the Lord your God with all your heart and with all your soul and with all your mind and with all your strength."

The Shema was the daily pray the Jews prayed in the morning and the evening. They began and ended their day with their focus on the supremacy of the Lord their God. It all begins and ends with Him. It was a declaration that there is only one divine, supreme Creator and He is Yahweh. This was in stark contrast to the many cultures and people that surrounded the Hebrews. The foreign cultures worshipped the gods of the harvest, the god of war, the sun and the moon, or the gods of the seasons. They were people who worshipped Egyptian, Greek, Roman, or pagan gods. It set the Hebrews apart from other nations for them to declare there is one God and He is not manipulated by offerings or sacrifices or man's whims. He is set apart and far above His creation.

When Jesus quoted the Sh'ma, His listeners immediately knew His meaning: there is one God and we are to worship Him with everything – our whole heart, soul, mind, and strength. This is the most important thing. He is the Center. No one in the crowd disagreed with Him. And then He listed the second most important commandment, to love our neighbor as ourselves. Even the teacher of the Law who asked the question knew what the right answer was supposed to be.

Jesus responded to what they already knew, there is an order. There are some things that are more important than other things and it starts with the Lord God. We are to love Him with everything we are. We get it backwards when we love ourselves first. When we start at that end (love our neighbor as *ourselves)* our lives get off track. It starts with and revolves around Him.

In the beginning God
created the heavens and the earth.
(Genesis 1:1)

Depression and anxiety distort our focus. It becomes too easy to focus on us and our worries, our discomfort, our frustrations, our fears, or our pain. Those annoying intrusive issues can become our focus, our primary focus. And some of those are real concerns. We have real issues to deal with but they get moved into first place. God or God's will or God's truth are still there and still relevant *but...*

Rather than bringing these things to God, we often try to bring God into these things. Our priority or our focus becomes getting better rather than pursuing Him. We set His will aside and want Him to abide by our will. Sometimes the focus isn't even about getting better, we're just consumed with everything that is wrong. We know God, we love God *but*…

Depression, anxiety, resentment, and fear are all self-feeding; they cause us to keep doing what will keep them thriving. The more we serve them, the more they master us. We isolate ourselves, we sleep more or don't sleep at all, we eat more or eat so little it's unhealthy, we become stagnant and lethargic, we avoid interaction, or we dwell on negative, overwhelming, fearful thoughts. We give into the thoughts that others have wronged us, are out to get us, or they don't care about us. We believe the worst thing will happen or already has. Our priorities change.

We do things differently going through depression or dealing with anxiety. And some of it we feel like we can't help. We want to go to church *but* here are all of the reasons we can't. We want to go to the store *but* we know how we feel when we do. We want to go visit that person *but* we're not guaranteed how it will turn out. We want to get up and get dressed *but* then what would we do? It feels like we stopped driving the bus and fear or anxiety or depression have taken over.

God where are You in the midst of this? What are You saying to me? *"Hear, O Israel, the Lord our God, the Lord is one. Love the Lord your God with all your heart and with all your soul and with all your mind and with all your strength."* With all your heart - whether it's broken, wounded, crushed, abandoned, cold, or feels like stone, love the Lord your God with all your heart. This is the place to start. Priorities; putting things in order.

*" All the others gave what they'll
never miss; she gave extravagantly
what she couldn't afford
— she gave her all."*
(Mark 12:44 The Message)

A few verses later, in Mark 12, Jesus *"sat down opposite the treasury, and began observing how the people were putting money into the treasury; and many rich people were putting in large sums. A poor widow came and put in two small copper coins, which amount to a cent. Calling His disciples to Him, He said to them, 'Truly I say to you, this poor widow put in more than all the contributors to the treasury; for they all put in out of their surplus, but she, out of her poverty, put in all she owned, all she had to live on.'"* (Mark 12:41-44 NASB) She gave all she had and Jesus noticed. We don't really know her story. We don't know if she was in distress or pain. We do know that she didn't have much but gave it all.

*Trust in the Lord with all your heart
And do not lean
on your own understanding.
In all your ways acknowledge Him,
And He will make your paths straight.*
(Proverbs 3:5,6 NASB)

Father, if I allow my circumstances or my emotions to dictate how much I give, I will be too cautious, too self-focused, too insecure. Help me to give it all, to pursue You with my whole heart, with my all my soul, with my complete mind, and with every ounce of my strength. Can I allow You to be an all consuming fire in my life? Every day I have to keep coming back to You as the Center. Help me to be focused on one thing, not double-minded, but focused fully on You.

A Word of Hope for Today: Your God sees you; He knows where you are and what you are going through. He invites you to give your whole heart, not just a part. He knows the wounds and the struggle and the doubt and He invites you to bring your wounded-ness to Him.

Take the time to examine your heart, your priorities. What gets in the way of giving everything? Pride, fear, insecurity, exhaustion, sin, etc...?

Write out a list of your priorities – what is most important in your life. Then look at your checkbook, your schedule, or your calendar, how do these match up with what you want or say are your priorities? How does this match up with God's word? Track how often the word "*but...*" pops up when talking or thinking about your priorities, what needs to change, or what you really want. Are you saying or thinking one thing *but* doing something different?

Going on from that place, he went into their synagogue, and a man with a shriveled hand was there. Looking for a reason to bring charges against Jesus, they asked him, " Is it lawful to heal on the Sabbath?" He said to them, " If any of you has a sheep and it falls into a pit on the Sabbath, will you not take hold of it and lift it out? How much more valuable is a person than a sheep! Therefore it is lawful to do good on the Sabbath." Then he said to the man, " Stretch out your hand." So he stretched it out and it was completely restored, just as sound as the other. But the Pharisees went out and plotted how they might kill Jesus.
Matthew 12:9-14

Church audiences can be tough. The religious leaders were trying to trap Jesus so when He side-stepped their trap, they plotted to kill Him. I hope we're a little more gracious today.

The religious leaders had transformed the standard for holiness that God had set up and had come up with their own standards. There was no room for grace. It was based on good works and outward appearances judged by them. In one sense they were trying to uphold the Law that had been passed down to them but they had distorted it and centered it around man rather than God. They reinforced the belief that if we do enough of the right things, God will be happy with us.

He taught as one who had authority, and not as their teachers of the law.
(Matthew 7:29)

The priests had allowed their faith to become a very man-centered approach. God had given them the Law with restrictions and rules. He had called them to live lives set apart from the surrounding cultures because they served a God who is set apart. Jesus stole their thunder as He went against what had been established and yet His actions still seemed to be in line with God. The people could hear it in His teachings. They knew He spoke with authority.

The Pharisees and Sadducees upheld the Law. They were entrusted to instruct and model what it meant to be faithful to God's Law. In trying to uphold the Law, they came up with their own rules to make it more practical but they skewed what God had intended. We have experienced ways of doing this today. We come up with our picture of what a good, faithful Christian looks like and then we judge who doesn't meet up to our standard. In the past, the church has come up with rules about dancing, music, make-up, clothes, church attendance, etc.. in an effort to help us obey God but then it becomes more about doing "the right thing" than it is about honoring God.

> *"it is not the healthy*
> *who need a doctor,*
> *but the sick."*

(Luke 5:31)

In Scripture, the only people Jesus criticized were the religious people. He called them a brood of vipers and pointed out how they were more concerned with looking good on the outside than the condition of their hearts (Mt 23). But, He reached out to sinners. He had a clear message of "sin no more" but He connected with them. The Pharisees asked why He was often seen eating or talking with the sinners and tax collectors (Mk 2:16, Lk 5:30). Jesus responded to that, *"it is not the healthy who need a doctor, but the sick."* (Lk 5:31) Sinners who know they are in need know that Jesus can help. The priests relied on their system for them to be ok.

The Law wasn't bad; it is good. But, the Law does not save us. Abiding by all of the rules does not make us more holy. The Law teaches us that we are sinful, we need to be saved, and we cannot do it on our own. Holiness is a high standard. The Jews were waiting for the Messiah, the Promised One who would deliver their people. The priests didn't believe it could be a simple, uneducated carpenter from Galilee. They knew His parents; they knew where He was from. He didn't match up with their standard or their perception of what He was supposed to look like.

The religious leaders tried to trap Jesus; they

plotted against Him, they tried to turn the people against Him, and they conspired to kill Him. He didn't fit in with how they conducted the Law. They erroneously had enforced a system that could save no one. They inadvertently taught the people to trust in their good works, to do the right things in the right way to be accepted by God.

This approach also bolstered the perception from the other angle: if bad things are happening, God must not be happy with us. It's not much different from superstition or ancient religious practices that appeased the gods so there would be victory in battle or a plentiful harvest. Jesus showed the people a different way.

> " How much more valuable
> is a person than a sheep! "
> (Matthew 12:12)

Standards and expectations can create a lot of anxiety. Especially when they are irrational expectations. The bar is set and then we have to get over the bar without touching it. And if we do touch it, look out. We can create anxiety by coming up with our own rules or expectations about God, life, love, people, or ourselves. Some of these expectations are misguided or twisted perceptions of the truth. We set up our rules for how we are supposed to be treated, how things are supposed to happen, what people should think of us, or even what it means to be a "good" Christian. We can get angry, irritable, inpatient, fearful, greedy, selfish, hypersensitive, or resentful when these expectations aren't met. Or, we may turn it into questions of why this is happening, why us, why now, does God love us, or why is He not doing more? We leave very little room for grace.

Our irrational or false standards and expectations set us up for tension or failure. Jesus shows us a better way. He tells us not to be anxious. Not because bad things will not happen but because our sufficiency is in Him. We can find our rest and peace in Him. We tell ourselves we don't deserve it so we try to earn it but that doesn't really work. He tells us we don't deserve it but His grace is sufficient for us. We can't do everything perfectly and His call to us is to be holy. We are only made holy in Him and by Him. He pursues after us. He first loved us. He reconciled us back to Himself. We are reliant on grace for salvation; can we be reliant on His grace in our everyday lives?

In this passage, Jesus showed compassion and mercy on the man with the withered hand. The Pharisees challenged Him on this. They wanted to stick with their rules for the Sabbath and their interpretation. He responded by healing the man. They challenged Him even before he healed. Apparently, they knew He was able to do it and wanted to catch Him doing something wrong. They ignored the fact that the hand was healed and God was moving. At other times, they accused Jesus of being empowered by the devil (Mt 9, Mt 12). They also asked Him for signs to show that He was sent by God. As they saw the signs, they excused away the truth and chose *their* methods. They were trying to be obedient but missed who the Law was suppose to connect them to. They were more focused on being right than knowing God or being compassionate. No room for grace.

Father, help me to not miss You. Don't let me get in the way. I want to see You move in power and for You to be glorified. Help me to be sensitive to what You are doing in my life and the lives of those around me. Help me to allow room for grace. Calm my anxious thoughts when I begin pressuring myself to achieve my standards. I would rather live by Your rules than mine. I can't achieve Your standard of holiness I can only trust in the blood of Jesus to cleanse me from all unrighteousness and put me in right standing with You.

A Word of Hope for Today: Your Heavenly Father treasures you. He finds value and worth in You. (He thinks you are more valuable than a sheep.) Rather than trying to keep up with all of your self-imposed rules or expectations, trust in the work of Christ. Know that your value and worth are found in Him, not in how good others think you are. Be intentional to write out a list of what you consider holy or good or good enough. Be honest with yourself, don't write out what you would tell someone; write out what standards you actually practice. Compare or contrast these with scripture. Throughout the day, catch your thoughts if you revert back to those standards.

Day 40

Therefore Jesus said again, "Very truly I tell you, I am the gate for the sheep. All who have come before me are thieves and robbers, but the sheep have not listened to them. I am the gate; whoever enters through me will be saved. They will come in and go out, and find pasture. The thief comes only to steal and kill and destroy; I have come that they may have life, and have it to the full." I am the good shepherd. The good shepherd lays down his life for the sheep. The hired hand is not the shepherd and does not own the sheep. So when he sees the wolf coming, he abandons the sheep and runs away. Then the wolf attacks the flock and scatters it. The man runs away because he is a hired hand and cares nothing for the sheep."

John 10:7-13

He will not abandon us. He is the good Shepherd. We can trust in Him to get us through what we are going through. Jesus spoke these words to the Pharisees. At first they didn't get it. He explained it again. The direction they were leading the people was not towards life and hope. They were the thieves and robbers He described. The thief comes to steal, kill, and destroy. He came to give us life, new life in Him.

> " I am the good shepherd;
> and I know My sheep,
> and am known by My own."
> (John 10:14 NKJV)

Our hope will always be in Him. He will lead us to safety; He will lead us to green pastures; He will lead us through the darkness; He will lead us beside still waters; He will lead us through the valley of the Shadow of Death; He will lead us along paths of righteousness. He will not abandon us or lead us astray. He laid down His life to keep us safe. He does not run at the first sign of trouble or difficulty.

As our good Shepherd, He is different from the hired hand who runs when danger or difficulty steps in. The hired hand doesn't care about the sheep, he is concerned with his own well-being. Jesus cares about His sheep. We are His. He has already laid down His life for us.

> " ...he goes on ahead of them,
> and his sheep follow him
> because they know his voice."
> (John 10:4)

The sheep know their shepherd's voice. Real shepherds are careful in how they speak. The sheep perk up and pay attention when they hear his voice because it means they are on the move or about to eat or there is danger. The shepherd talks quietly when not talking to the sheep. But when He speaks they listen. The sheep know the shepherd's voice because he spends his life with them day after day. He puts himself in harm's way to protect their lives and to care for them. We know our Shepherd's voice when we spend time with Him in prayer, in His word, and in fellowship with other believers. We learn to distinguish His voice from false shepherds or the voice of the world. He leads us to green pastures; He restores our souls. The world offers something different than a restored soul; the world entices us with riches or fame or security or popularity. He offers us peace and joy and hope and eternal security. When we follow after the wrong voice, we end up in the wrong pasture where our souls are not fed or restored or protected.

The voice of depression or anxiety can lead us astray. We can find ourselves desperately running around trying to find peace or joy or strength or security. Depression has a way of twisting the truth, leading us to believe it's all bad, it will never get better, or there is no hope. When we know His voice, we can rest securely knowing that whatever we are facing He is more than able to handle. The wolf will attack; the lion will sneak in. Will we run in fear or find our strength in Him? Can we find our strength in His strength? Will we listen to His voice to know how to respond? We can rest in His goodness.

Jesus didn't just describe Himself as a shepherd, but as the good Shepherd. The Pharisees understood the contrast He made as he called them thieves and robbers who came to steal and kill and then the description of Himself as good. They understood He was not alluding to his adept ability to shepherd real sheep but an innate goodness that He said they lacked. He is good. Culturally, they also understood no one is good except God and here Jesus claimed to be good with good intentions. His sheep could trust Him because He is good. This is why we hear in verse 31 the Pharisees picked up rocks to stone Him because He claimed to be good; He claimed to be God.

> " *I am the good shepherd.*
> *The good shepherd*
> *lays down his life*
> *for the sheep.* "
> (John 10:11)

Because He is good, we can trust Him with whatever we are going through. In spite of what is happening, we can trust in His goodness. It may not feel good. We may be going through the worst trials of our lives but our assurance is, *"I give them eternal life, and they shall never perish; no one will snatch them out of my hand."* (John 10:28) What you are going through may be a struggle. It may be difficult to hear that He has an eternal perspective when your physical or emotional or mental state is hurting right here right now. The relief you are looking for may feel like it is beyond your grasp. Listen for His voice. He will lead you through it. Trust in His goodness.

Is your God too small? Do you doubt His ability to get you through this? Can you believe He is more than able to overcome your current situation? Are you more focused on avoiding this than accepting that He is with you and will go through this with you? Listen for His voice, what is He saying to you? Do you trust in His goodness? Can you believe that He wants what is best for you and allows you to grow through the difficult times?

As you come to the end of these 40 days, are you in a different place from where you started? Have you committed to changing you rather than the struggling through the frustration of trying to change everyone else? Are you experiencing more peace or joy or strength as you press on through your circumstances? Do you believe He is restoring and refreshing your soul?

The Lord is my shepherd, I shall not want.

(Psalm 23:1 NASB)

Father, You are good. You are faithful. Help me to keep my eyes on You rather than my circumstances. Help me to hear Your voice above the voices around me or the struggles within me. Help me to know Your voice from these other voices calling to me. Where there may be confusion or stress or fear, replace it with your peace. Where there may be doubt or weakness, replace it with your strength. Where there may be darkness or sadness or loneliness, replace it with Your joy. Where there may be hopelessness or regret, replace it with Your hope. Let my life and my choices glorify You and be a testimony or Your great love.

A Word of Hope for Today: Commit to spending time daily in prayer and the Word of God. Reach out to others and connect in fellowship and encouragement. Continue to challenge the thoughts that are working against you. Be active daily. Allow yourself to have fun and laugh. Be aware of what is going on physically, emotionally, mentally, relationally, and spiritually. Continue to take small steps and moving in the direction you want to end up. As you run the race, keep your eyes on the author and perfecter of your faith.

I want to know Christ—yes, to know the power of his resurrection and participation in his sufferings, becoming like him in his death, and so, somehow, attaining to the resurrection from the dead. Not that I have already obtained all this, or have already arrived at my goal, but I press on to take hold of that for which Christ Jesus took hold of me. Brothers and sisters, I do not consider myself yet to have taken hold of it. But one thing I do: Forgetting what is behind and straining toward what is ahead, I press on toward the goal to win the prize for which God has called me heavenward in Christ Jesus. (Philippians 3:10-14)

38742090R00135

Made in the USA
Middletown, DE
26 December 2016